DI025387

MARKETING
AND
SELLING
DESIGN
SERVICES

MARKETING
AND
SELLING
DESIGN
SERVICES

The Designer
Client Relationship

MARY V. KNACKSTEDT
ASID • IFDA

with Laura J. Haney

 VAN NOSTRAND REINHOLD
_____ New York

Library of Congress Catalog Card Number 92-5392
ISBN 0-442-01073-7

Printed in the United States of America.

Van Nostrand Reinhold
115 Fifth Avenue
New York, New York 10003

Chapman and Hall
2-6 Boundary Row
London, SE1 8HN, England

Thomas Nelson Australia
102 Dodds Street
South Melbourne 3205
Victoria, Australia

Nelson Canada
1120 Birchmount Road
Scarborough, Ontario MIK 5G4, Canada

16 15 14 13 12 11 10 9 8 7 6 5 4 3 2 1

Library of Congress Cataloging-in-Publication Data

Knackstedt, Mary V.
    Marketing and selling design services : the designer/client
relationship / Mary V. Knackstedt, with Laura J. Haney.
        p.   cm.
    Includes bibliographical references and index.
    ISBN 0-442-01073-7 : $29.95
        1. Interior decoration firms—United States—Management.
    2. Design services—United States—Marketing.   I. Haney, Laura J.
    II. Title.
    NK2116.2.K58   1992
    729'.068'8—dc20   92-5392
                                                                            CIP

CONTENTS

Contents

PREFACE

There is no easy way, no quick fix, for building and maintaining a quality relationship. Designer-client relationships are the same. However, there are procedures and systems that have been tried and proved effective.

This book presents many of them.

They are all designed with the position of the designer as the key.

After all, we are not the same as our clients. We don't want to be, and they don't want us to be. But we do need to realize that we have the ability and the need to build strong relationships with people of many different orientations.

Psychologists have shown us many methods for directing our communication efforts so they are understood by people who think differently from ourselves. This book is based on simple, easy processes that are constantly at work building and enriching that relationship that bonds a "best" client with a "best" designer.

This kind of a relationship is based on teamwork with the client, sitting on their side of the table, working with them. They buy—we don't sell. The relationship is cooperative, helpful, sensitive. It has many variables. We must keep the structure for this freedom so that we can accomplish our objectives. Every form or process is created to keep us on track so that we are constantly aware of mutual goals.

This book will give you pointers and details that will help develop your expertise and help you to relate to the client—the essence of any design practice. It addresses the particular needs of the design discipline, calling on talents, abilities and tools available to a design firm.

The marketing and selling procedures and processes described here are designed to complement the practice of interior design, and call on talents and abilities you already have. It is a proactive approach that turns everyday issues into marketing and sales development opportunities.

As you review and plan your company's strategy, consider and concentrate on:

- Responding to clients. What are their needs, desires, and wants? How can you best communicate and manage this process? They are our partners—they come first.
- Using your resources, staff, and sources with respect and care.
- Creating opportunities that allow you to demonstrate the best possible design using products in the correct places.
- Giving talented staff the opportunity to grow and develop and shine. Creativity grows and blossoms with success.
- Complete projects as efficiently as you can. Time is all we have. We must respect both our own and our client's time. Review the project. Plan the time schedule as you design the job. Be sure the schedule fits the client.

PART 1

EFFECTIVE MARKETING STRATEGIES

Chapter 1

Positioning Your Firm

Today, design firms need to think about how we present ourselves. Presentation is the basis for what we call business development. We talk about this in the form of marketing and selling design services. Marketing comprises all the activities that build the relationship between the designer and client, including product development, research and promotion. Selling is a process of educating and communicating directly with potential buyers. It begins when you attract their attention and continues through developing their interest and giving them the information that helps them evaluate the decision. It ends with the commitment.

Just as McDonald's learned to sell hamburgers and hospitals learned to sell medicine, interior designers need to learn to market and sell design services. And this probably won't be easy, as most of us have a built-in aversion to selling. The word has so many negative connotations. I don't want to sell or to persuade. I want to educate and communicate with clients to help them make informed choices; I want to turn wants and even some whims into needs.

Designers need to develop techniques of communicating

effectively with the particular client group we seek. The firm that knows how to market and how to communicate is most likely to get the business.

A designer's business is to solve problems that the client cannot or does not want to solve alone. It is the designer's job to identify the problem and through technical skill and expertise, demonstrate our ability to solve problems. To sell our services, interior designers must show that we are business people who understand construction, scheduling and budgets.

It is up to us to educate the consumer through marketing. Only an informed consumer can differentiate between partial service and full service, unqualified and qualified designers. Designers like to believe that they can rely on referrals as their major marketing tool. But any informed firm knows that this is no longer enough. Established firms can lose jobs to inexperienced newcomers to the field who have sophisticated techniques to market their design skills.

In order to be effective, market development must be a highly systematized, structured process, with exact schedules, measurements and reviews of each part of the process—from defining your market and making the first contact, through to writing proposals into production and following up.

The purpose of the marketing plan is to help your firm focus directly on the type of work that is most profitable and appropriate for it. It is also designed to help you understand what you are, what you really want and how to attain your goals. After all, as a designer, you want to create your own destiny. You don't want to sit there and wait for something to happen; chances are that what happens won't be right. You want to design your firm to enhance your chances for success. Obtaining the wrong business doesn't really develop a design studio; it can only destroy it.

What does it really take to devise a program that is profitable and directly related to securing the appropriate business for your firm?

First, what projects are appropriate? A big part of marketing is defining what type of work is best for your firm, and refining that definition as your market changes. You need to think about who you are. You need to analyze your values, systems, mission, and exactly where you want to be.

And you must look at who your client is. Any good program is a partnership or marriage between a client and a firm with capabilities which match or complement that client's needs. It is a mistake to place your entire emphasis on existing or prospective clients and overlook inhouse capabilities.

BUILDING YOUR DEFINITION

In the design field, each of us comes from a different background, a different school, a different part of the country. We have aptitudes in many varied areas. Some of us are involved with very technical work and very detailed contract specifications. Others are doing highly inventive work. Each of these different design disciplines has its own management requirements. Each specialty has its own vocabulary, so the process must be designed to meet its requirements.

Your marketing plan helps you set a direction. It is essential to approaching the right kind of client. It also helps you to minimize day-to-day problems. If you are going in 74 directions, you cannot be effective or achieve professional results. You—and everyone who works with you—need to understand your goals and where you are going, in order to work toward the same direction. Mutual understanding will eliminate a good deal of confusion. Directed firms don't waste as much time with crisis management.

With a proactive, progressive approach, you spend time directing, staying on track, and, therefore, achieve greater results. You are also able to maximize your own potential. In some instances, this progressive approach may require a firm to alter its qualifications and, to some extent, retrain the staff. But at least you know what the needs are, because you have explored them with your clients.

The most effective way to get to achieve your goals is to create a map (Multiple Action Plan). Figure out where you want to be and decide upon the best ways to get there. As you work on your marketing plan, it is important to focus on your abilities and your resources, to consider how you can relate to your client, and offer the best possible project. The ability to produce good quality jobs efficiently and with an effective price is the key to building a strong client base today.

For a marketing plan to be valuable, a regular schedule and dedication are required. You must act consistently, not just when business is poor, so that you get the results you want. This is the excitement of a good marketing plan: It provides your firm with opportunities . . . opportunities that would not exist otherwise. It gives you the chance to create your future.

A marketing plan takes both management and leadership. Every person with the firm, starting with the CEO, must be dedicated to this plan. In addition, someone must manage the plan's direction, to make sure that every phone call, networking system, meeting, or whatever bridging systems you use, is accomplished. Each person in the firm must be involved; some will be with responsibilities for specific processes.

You need a specific structure to ensure your firm operates productively. Building a client base requires consistency. Be sure you are able to fulfill any commitments you make, otherwise you will neither be able to build your clients' trust nor make these marketing systems work. Select your actors and direct their roles with flair.

SUCCESSFUL DESIGN FIRMS

Today's successful firms are very heavily market driven. They are based on what the clients need and want to purchase. Those firms understand exactly how their clients perceive their firm and how they perceive their needs. Design firms that spend time researching and developing a client find it easier to obtain, produce and complete projects. A great deal of time is invested in this process, and it pays off a hundred-fold.

Take into account that it costs you five times as much to attract a new client as it does to retain an existing one. A client who has worked with you before knows about your firm, knows your strengths and knows exactly how to work with you. You stand a greater chance of winning a good, profitable job from an existing client than from a new one.

Very few firms can operate up to capacity without a marketing program. You need an ongoing program, most likely led by the chief executive officer, especially in the smaller firms. The leader must see this as his or her most important job, and be ready to dedicate whatever it takes to make the program work. If you work alone, and many of us do, you need to dedicate a portion of your time each week to marketing. For example, you may simply set aside two hours each morning for working on the marketing program before attending to anything else. If your firm is large enough, you may be able to assign the day-to-day management of the program to someone else.

Consider the current trends. We are in a very service-oriented period, a period when even the best-known design firms must invest in sales development to maintain their shares of the market. Projects are awarded to firms that handle a need, firms that understand clients and are willing to be part of their teams.

The goal is to build longterm relationships with clients. A different type of presentation and a different type of staffing are required to achieve that goal. To build a good client base, your entire strategy must be client-oriented. If you are putting all your time into new client development each month, you're in trouble. It takes five times as much money and effort to develop a new client as it does to maintain an existing one. The question is, how can we develop our existing clients and keep them, and how can we continue to make this business profitable?

Let's look at who needs what we are able to provide. Not everyone needs or wants our services, in which case we'd better find another client. Who is looking for what we have? Who is making strong changes? What are the geographic limitations for managing the type of work we do best? What production methods and details should be considered? You must answer these questions before defining the "best" client.

Success in this marketplace calls for ability, understanding, planning, and maintenance.

Interior designers need basic technical ability backed up by good resources and by staff who know how to complete a job successfully without too many problems.

We must understand our market, our clients. What are they all about? What are their particular likes, desires and interests? What do they want from us?

We must have a plan in order to reach those clients, a method of bridging, of building a link between our staff and our clients. Once built, the link needs constant maintenance. We must adhere to a consistent schedule for contact of clients and prospective clients so that we see them eye-to-eye, person-to-person, as often as possible. Clients don't want distant design experts today; they want designers who understand their special needs and who are ready to respond.

The reasons for buying architecture, engineering and all areas of design services have changed considerably. In the seventies and early eighties, clients looked for the firm that could produce the most creative job. Now the most important attribute of a design firm is the ability to finish the job on time and within budget. Often budgets for large contracts are established before a design firm is interviewed. Design professionals are asked to team up with contractors to provide the owner with a single contract for a complete project at this pre-established price.

Success as designers isn't simply how creative we are, but how well we understand the complete discipline and whether we can deliver this highly technical knowledge well and efficiently, both financially and in time-structure. It isn't just the beauty of the design that matters, but whether we can deliver it efficiently and economically.

Most clients like to hire someone that they already know and trust; the investment is heavy, and the project is important to them. Building that rapport and developing that communication system with the client is very important, and it must start long before that job is awarded.

The system of communication described in *Marketing and Selling Design Services* has several key elements. You must understand your abilities as a design team, including the production abilities of your sources. You must research and define the best client group for your firm, then specifically select that target group and develop a bridging system. Many of these systems are presented in the section on bridging techniques, including advertising and promotion, networking, and other ways of acquainting yourself with these people and creating a bridge between the right firm and the right client.

I think you can see that building your marketing program doesn't stop when you win the project. It continues throughout the job in the way you present yourself, the way each staff member relates to clients, and how well they do their jobs. The paper hanger out on your project is either enhancing your firm's reputation or destroying your job.

There are many ways to develop your lifestyle to complement your marketing program. Everything you do, from where and how you live, to your hobbies and where you do your grocery shopping, affects your position as a designer.

FOCUS YOUR MARKET

Focusing on a particular segment of the overall market improves a firm's chances for positioning and success; this way the firm can concentrate on acquiring the best clients, and using its talents to the greatest potential. For instance, have you thought about what your firm will need in terms of outside human and material resources, consultants, other professionals, and products?

Focusing increases efficiency: Once you know where you are going, you can direct your energies accordingly making your firm more able to compete for work that might not have been attainable previously. The commitment to competitiveness is stimulating—the staff reaps greater rewards.

To limit the costs of your marketing efforts, confine your market area to those individuals or organizations that need what your firm can provide.

SUCCESS

Success in business is based on:

1. The client. The client comes first: he or she wants what he or she wants, and if you can't do it, there are plenty of others out there who will.
2. Communication ability. Most of the ability to develop your position in a company situation depends on your ability to communicate. This may mean many things. Throughout this book you will see many very simple everyday issues addressed because it is often the simple everyday issues such as a lack of clear communication that build or destroy a job. Sometimes we forget or just don't think these small things are noticed. They, like housework, are most noticeable in their absence . . . when you don't provide the expected, you hear about it. Even if you feel your methods of communication are fine, compare them to others in the field. Maybe there is a standard way of doing things.

In some of the more artistic (not strictly functional) areas of design you could do something wrong and no one would ever know the difference. But in more functional areas of design, such as space planning, one deviation from the norm, and the client thinks there is something wrong, whether there is or not.
3. Teamwork. We cannot work alone and accomplish the masterful level of design work we all desire. We must be able to build the appropriate team to complete the job. This takes many levels of experience. It also requires consideration, and an understanding of a team's various crafts and disciplines. The interior designer is the design coordinator. So just like an orchestra leader, we must be sure everyone is playing the same music.

4. Speed. Today most people expect fast results. We must be able to produce jobs faster. This is what our clients expect. It is too expensive to do it any other way.

5. Change. This is the only thing you can count on. Fortunately interior design is based on change. Each part of your work and career will be constantly in the process of redesign. Fortunately we were trained for this. This is part of the character of interior design.

```
                    What I Want Our Business to Be


    1.     Our income is accomplished by providing these services


    2.     Type of projects


    3.    Our clients are


    4.    Staff


    5.    Income expected


    6.    Success is
```

Figure 1-1

	Hospitality	Health/Medical	Residential
AIM OF OUR PRACTICE:			
WHAT WE DO:			
OUR ACCOMPLISHMENTS:			
WITH OUR ABILITIES WE ARE GOING TO: (GOALS IN NEXT 3 YEARS):			
PRACTICAL GEOGRAPHIC RANGE TO WORK:			
TYPICAL SIZED PROJECTS:			
IF WE REACH OUR GOALS IN NEXT 3 YEARS WE WILL BE DOING			

Figure 1-2

	Hospitality	Health/Medical	Residential
AIM OF OUR PRACTICE:			
WHAT WE DO:	Design & specify only Design and supply parts	Turnkey (complete job)	Design & specify only Design and supply parts
OUR ACCOMPLISHMENTS:	Leader in hospitality	Great experience in nursing homes	Masters at Victorian restoration
WITH OUR ABILITIES WE ARE GOING TO: (GOALS IN NEXT 3 YEARS):	Expand to other countries Hotel chains	Work in retirement centers Nursing home chains Professionals with special interests	Do work with finer artists
PRACTICAL GEOGRAPHIC RANGE TO WORK:	Worldwide	Within 200 miles	Within 100 miles
TYPICAL SIZED PROJECTS:	$5 million to $1 billion	$100 to $500 million	$50,000 to $250,000
IF WE REACH OUR GOALS IN NEXT 3 YEARS WE WILL BE DOING	Exceptional high levels varied hotel owners	Projects for restort type residences for aging	High budget with antiques of special quality; publishable work

Figure 1-3. Sample filled-in form.

Chapter 2

The Marketing Plan

• GOALS •

Have the kind of work we do best.

Have the right clients.

Have consistent work throughout the year, or at least fewer highs and lows.

Increase our market shares.

Increase profit so that we can properly compensate the staff and acquire the equipment we need to develop and expand.

• AIM •

To accomplish your goals, yours, and not someone else's; own your career.

Learn from others. They know how they want to be treated.

Demonstrate sincere caring. This is worth more than anything you can buy.

Help your clients realize their great potential through appropriate interior design. Make them look great.

Realize the excitement of knowledge. Study and learn. Improvement and success starts with ability. Today it takes constant training.

Take the time necessary to build the proper relationships with clients. Only the right relationship will give you the basis for doing the right job.

Our consultants, sources, craftsmen are what make us. Without them we cannot do interior design.

Fortunately, you learned enough in school to get a job in design. Keeping that job depends on what you continue to learn from your present teachers, clients, consultants, sources, and craftspeople.

Commit to what it takes to create and carry out a successful marketing plan. You will need to define, on paper:

1. Your mission
2. Objectives
3. Value statement
4. Company's goals—results you want
5. Budget
6. Company profile—internal
    a. Staff experience and background
    b. Specialty
    c. Experience: past projects
    d. Past revenue sources
    e. Product: define what it is that you have to sell.
    f. Strengths and weaknesses
    g. Sales force

h. Income profile—past revenues and current expenses compared to the current market
7. The Marketplace—external
   a. Client profiles, current and potential
   b. Geographic limits
   c. Prospect list
   d. Resources: suppliers, crafts and trades
   e. Competition
   f. Economic conditions
   g. Social and cultural trends
   h. Legal, governmental and regulatory forces
   i. Technological issues
8. Market research
9. Compare your company profile and the market of potential clients. Define your best client.
10. Create a bridge between your firm and the best client.
11. Select a manager and a leader.
12. Create a map, a plan to make this happen.
13. Prepare needed materials.
14. Make it happen.
15. Measure results, make changes as needed.

BUDGET

Good market development requires that you spend at least a modest amount of money on promotional tools. How much should a public relations and marketing program cost? A minimum of three to five percent of your gross income, not gross sales.

If you are employed by a large practice which has its own budget for promotion, you should still dedicate five to ten percent of your gross income to promoting your career or your company as a design firm. For instance, you may have done an outstanding dental office project. The firm may choose not to publicize this even though the work is topnotch, because its interests are not in attracting more dental office business. You need to put money aside so that you can photograph your own work, or take a course that develops your specialty.

YOUR MISSION STATEMENT

A mission statement is basically a goal with a deadline. It is the foundation of your marketing plan.

Designers are often told that they are dreamers. As designers we know that dreaming is the first part of any accomplishment. The question is, how does this dream become a realizable mission, an achievable goal? As designers we can continue to survive, but surviving is not the highest level of creativity. The goal is to put your firm in a position that allows you to do truly creative work, and to take some of that creative passion and put it into practice.

To figure out where you want to be, decide who your heroes are. What can you learn from them? What are you aiming for? There are many really beautifully designed interior spaces, and some that we admire. How were these accomplished?

Build on what you admire, set yourself a goal, write your mission statement, and take steps to accomplish it. This mission must coordinate the demands of your lifestyle with those of your business.

Your mission very strongly directs how you conduct yourself throughout your business career. As you write and develop your mission, consider how it will affect the way you live, both as a designer, and personally.

The mission directs the activities of your firm's efforts. By clearly defining the objective of your practice, you establish what is needed to accomplish your mission. The mission states the aim of our practices—our basic orientation. This must be specifically defined in order to know how and where to position the firm within the market.

Your mission statement must be written down, and you will most likely change it many times until you get it just right. Your mission statement is not that you simply want to earn a living.

Define your business and its unique position in the design field. How are you different and superior? What is your competitive advantage?

You need to develop a focus. A major problem of interior design firms is a lack of focus. Too many firms are willing to take any type of work that comes along because it's interesting. That does not lead to a profitable business. You are going to have to look at your work and decide what is worth focusing on. What can you do which will retain your interest for a long period of time? What are you excited about doing?

The answer to these questions should be your specialty. And, if you are willing to take the energy to specialize, you will also become an expert in your field. You will be working with it every single day; soon you will know where all the problems are long before they occur, because this is your interest, this is your focus.

VALUES

The next statement you need is your value statement. For example, most designers will not undertake any work that does not adhere to the building codes of the state in which they live and work. Although certain BOCA (Building Officials and Code Administrators) codes may not be required in the area, the design firm may believe that they are important and will be required eventually. Therefore, their designs must meet those additional codes; they feel morally responsible to meet those standards.

Your next value decision may be that you will refuse a project that is not a good example of your type of work. For example, clients may ask you to do a type of project that has a purpose for them, but that does not fit your mission and your objects. You should be willing to turn that project down and to expend your energy trying to obtain the projects that are suitable for your firm.

Suppose your aim is to create the finest high technology rooms for audiovisual presentations. If a prospective client is unwilling to use the appropriate components, the project will not perform as well as it ought to. The space will not be a good example of your work. Control becomes a factor when you decide to use only equipment made by a certain manufacturer; cabinetry from one source, finishes from another. Because you need control to accomplish your goals, only turnkey jobs meet your standards.

DO WHAT YOU LOVE

What do you really care about? After years in the field you may tire of some kinds of projects. Regardless of who the client is, you won't be able to do your best because you can't put in the effort that the project requires and deserves. So review the project carefully to see whether you really care about this.

Do you like the client?
Are you interested in improving their situation?
Does the project have some purpose to it?
What is the most important part of the project?

Does the subject interest you? Are you excited about
learning more about it?

Do you want to invest time in this particular specialty?

Don't underestimate the importance of being excited
about your work. Creativity is exciting, stimulating,
and keeps you healthy. I feel so much better when I
am involved in a project with a high level of creativity
and some excitement. If a project excites you, it could
be right for your firm.

HOW GREAT DO YOU WANT YOUR PRACTICE TO BE?

A great firm is developed; it doesn't just happen. It's developed
by people who are looking at ordinary, everyday issues and
trying to find just one small way of making it better. You can't
make one item 100 percent better, but you can improve a
hundred different items by just one to three percent.

Look at your practice every day and ask yourself what
you can do to improve it. If you can afford to improve it,
make it happen. Giving your clients the best possible service
is how you build and maintain a practice. If you give your
best daily, your practice won't require any major changes or
revamping. It will gradually grow and progress with the need
and the direction of the field.

The clients will see that you're great and keep coming
back to you because they like you. They know that there is
some special aura about this practice. This is a practice that
really tries to service them. If they really enjoy being around
you, they're comfortable in investing with you, and this builds
higher budgets.

As Tom Peters has said many times, "We must stick to
our knitting." Staying close to our own field and getting closer
and closer to our clients builds a valuable practice.

Chapter 3

Objectives

What are your objectives? Do you want to produce a high quality project at a reasonable price? Perhaps your objective is to give the best quality of design within a particular specialty. A designer who specializes in penal institutions and public spaces has different objectives from the person whose work appeals to the emotions, such as residential work or some types of marketing and executive spaces.

The basic objective is to practice the discipline of interior design while earning an appropriate income to support yourself, and to meet the expenses of staff and office. Beyond that, you may believe that your design work can improve the quality of people's lives. Is your objective to present a specific design style? To enrich people's lives? To solve space problems?

One of your key objectives should be a deep commitment to communicating the opportunities of design through the process of marketing, and building a relationship with the potential buyer.

There are usually two major reasons for any marketing program. One is to develop a higher profit within your projects. Secondly, you want to gain more of the market share—not necessarily a larger share of the market, but a better share of the market, one that is more appropriate to your firm.

If volume is your objective, you need to determine how much and where. You don't want to add confusion, but you want to add specific, defined growth. To do so, you must be able to take on and manage this larger volume successfully.

QUALITY

One marketing goal is improved quality. All of our clients like to hear that effort is made to improve work or products. The design world is one of constant change, and our clients enjoy seeing these improvements.

Quality is very often totally independent of cost. The fact that something is good does not necessarily mean that it is expensive. The quality of an item can depend on its suitability for the particular project.

Quality isn't always a question of giving a client a good product; it's a question of our ability to produce a quality design at an effective price. This most often relates to the way we produce the job. Is there a way to simultaneously improve the quality of the design and to achieve a product that will be good for a long period? For instance, one firm has chosen "less is less" as its motto. This means the firm has chosen to work for fewer clients, and to do it right the first time. There will be less waste of time, materials and energy—all in all, a more exacting art.

To achieve quality work and produce it at effective prices, designers need to acquire and keep the very best possible people for their studios. We need first to determine the components of good performance and what results are expected on the job, and then to let our staff do it. Let them be creative. Create an atmosphere in which your staff can work efficiently and well.

Specialization and repetition can teach you the shortcuts that allow you to achieve higher quality with less effort and aggravation. Increased volume in purchasing certain products often means quantity discounts that can be passed along to the client. Is there a way to design your practice so that it is oriented to both quality and production—so that you can give your client a better product at an economical price?

PROFIT

One goal of a marketing plan is to increase profits. There are two primary ways to do this.

1. Increase the total sale or amount of income secured by the design firm.
2. Increase the amount of profit or markup. It isn't enough to simply increase sales; you need to keep track of the percentage of profit on each particular job.

This is as much the basis of marketing as of any other financial program. Growth is really the key to profit for many business endeavors. The future of a company depends on its flexibility and willingness to grow. Decide whether you should become larger, smaller, or stay the same size. Decide which is the most profitable direction for your company.

CONSIDERATION

Let's look at how designers make money. We expect designers who secure multi-million dollar projects to have formidable incomes and wonderful opportunities. Some practices that you'd expect to be the most profitable are actually among the least profitable.

Why? On these multi-million dollar projects, there are large numbers of people involved. Yet today, the average budget for office space is roughly $250 per square foot—of which only five dollars is allotted to cover all design services. These include architecture, engineering, all the specialists and consultants called in on the project, and, of course, the interior designer.

Think of the amount of liability and control and management that is purchased for five dollars a square foot and you will see the problem. There is a problem whenever you have a lot of responsibility for a low amount of money. Interior designers are responsible for the entire multi-million dollar project, yet the total budget for all design services is one-fiftieth of the project budget.

At one time, budgets for design services were much higher but the current competitive market limits what we can charge. Unless you offer a service or product that is unique or different, you can only charge what other people are charging. Clients know the charge per square foot on a given project. You must bid with caution to be sure that your amounts fall within the accepted range.

This means that the only way to achieve higher income levels is to make your firm's services unique. One way is to become a specialist, to develop your practice in such a way that no one else can install that type of job as well, and as easily, as you can. Being a specialist makes it price effective.

Some of our ability to produce quality design work at an effective price depends on our resources. In seminars when I asked design professionals to rate the products and services in our industry, I was shocked at the level of dissatisfaction. Often, designers did not feel that they had the appropriate products available. They did not feel that resource companies were ready or willing to stand behind them in the event of a problem with the merchandise.

Interior designers need to be able to control situations. We need to know that our resources will ship the quality products we order, when we need them. Especially when we have projects that stretch our abilities, we need to know that the factory is behind us and is ready to make the necessary changes.

When design professionals create something truly unusual, it almost always works best in a design-build situation, where the factory is close at hand and works intimately with the designer. If there is a problem, it can be solved on the spot immediately.

On larger projects where everything is specified in detail and must be bid, it is often necessary to use standard items. Too much creativity can cause problems on certain kinds of projects. (Hospitality design, for instance, demands a certain amount of creativity to provide that signature look.) The dealership that is awarded the bid may decide to substitute, or the factory may say it can't be done as specified. The end product is not what you planned, and you have a problem where four items don't properly coordinate.

I asked hospitality design specialists what percentage of the job was actually produced exactly as they *thought* they had specified it. They said that if they hit sixty percent, they were delighted.

Well, in many situations sixty percent accuracy is not enough. You want and need more precision, but if sixty percent accuracy is all that is expected, can you design your projects to allow for this?

If you are specifying hundreds of thousands of dollars, or multi-million dollar projects, you need to consider the purchasing and delivery process among the many variables. Will that project be completed within the time allotted and within the specifications if you add some creativity? Unless you know and can work within the capabilities of your vendors, the answer is probably not because the job is too large.

These aspects of design are important when you design your company profile. You must decide how creative you are able to be within the limitations of the types of work you do. What are you realistically able to offer your clients?

Create your program using methods and suggestions in this book. Choose techniques that fit your chosen clientele, and use the ones that are most comfortable for your firm. To keep your commitment high, you and your staff must be able to accomplish and succeed, and feel good about yourselves. So map out a schedule that is possible within the realm of your company's capabilities.

Chapter 4

Company Profile/Internal

In the design field, each of us comes from a different background, a different school, a different part of the country. We have aptitudes in many areas. Some of us deal with very technical work and very detailed contract specifications. Others are doing highly inventive work. Before you begin your marketing program, you need to be aware of the skills and abilities within the firm. These are what distinguish your firm different; they are what you have to communicate with your marketing plan.

WHAT ARE YOU BEST AT?

Look at yourself. What is the best thing you do, and what are your personal limitations? Design your career around these two factors. If you're a person who loves details, fine, make sure that you do the detail work. If this is something that you prefer to skip over, remember that it is still a necessary part of the interior design profession and hire someone else to take over this responsibility.

Review past projects in terms of accomplishment and

satisfaction. Make a list of what you do best, and keep it beside you as you consider new projects. When you hit a client situation that is really not within the range of what you or your firm should be doing, either bring in a consultant or possibly refer the project to someone else. Accepting a project that is too far beyond your range can destroy your company, seriously affect your profits, and jeopardize the entire project. We can't do everything well; do what you do best.

BEST TYPE OF STAFF FOR YOUR FIRM

Interior designers so often hire the person with similar training and abilities; this may not be the best person to hire. You need someone who is talented in skills you lack. Some of the most successful organizations are based on teams, with one person who is very much a designer, highly creative and very much into all the details of design; another team member who is really into communicating and presenting projects; and a third who enjoys managing the business.

Is your current staff oriented toward your firm's direction? You may have to replace staff members to achieve your goals.

Every person on your staff represents your firm in their every action. Build your staff and your group of consultants with the best possible people that you can find. Strong people complement other strong people. If they're not qualified, they only pull the rest of the group down.

You want people who are reasonably bright and intelligent. It's much easier to work with them, and if you're a very bright person you may find it very difficult to get along with people who aren't reasonably smart. Second, find people who are well educated, both as a result of schooling and of learning by doing.

Anyone you hire should have a good basic character. Do a credit check as well as a character check. Find out as much as you can because the way they manage their lives affects their ability to do well in your firm.

Is this person compatible with the people in your firm, and with your clients? Sometimes people who perform well don't fit your style of working. In a small firm, you will be working together constantly. There must be some camaraderie; you have to be able to get along.

Finally, because the field of interior design requires a lot of effort and long hours, it is important to find someone who has the energy to put into the field. Energy is the single most important characteristic of a successful person. If they have too many outside interests, they may not have the time nor the energy to dedicate to the design practice. Are they willing to exert the kind of energy it takes to make it happen?

DESIGN STAFF QUESTIONNAIRE

Now let's look at your staff. Exactly what type of designers or specialists are they? You need to know as much about them as possible. What do they bring to your firm? How can you best present them as professionals? Ask each of them to fill out the Design Staff Questionnaire.

Using the Design Staff Questionnaire, ask each employee for an update every six months, and keep the completed forms in your business development file. Don't forget to fill one out yourself! The questionnaire asks the staff person to look at his or her education and experience in terms of what was accomplished or learned. You need specific information, so the more precise a staffer is, the more useful the form will be in your assessment of the capabilities of your firm. Once the profiles are completed, go over them and determine what the staff people have done within their past work experiences.

Where was the person educated and what degree was earned? Was the school in the East or the West; was it a specialized school with a particular emphasis, such as historical preservation, contemporary design, or barrier-free environments? What is his or her particular emphasis?

What courses were studied, when, and what was learned or accomplished? Sometimes we take a particular course for a reason, perhaps because of an outstanding professor. The course may have been misnamed; you thought it was going to be dedicated to one issue but it turned out to emphasize another. Outline what special things were learned from that course.

If the staff person received awards, what are they and how did he or she earn them? Was it a solo project or done as part of a group?

What other education has he or she received? This can include seminars, lectures, workshops. Again, you want to know the subject, the dates attended, and what was learned or accomplished. Has he or she served as an apprentice, or participated in volunteer programs?

The second page details employment experience. In addition to the name of the companies, positions held and the dates, what was the on-the-job experience? In conducting this type of interview or review, I find there is often a great deal of difference between the title of a job and what it actually entails. I think we need to look at the person not only in the light of where he or she worked, but also for exactly what they did and what they learned in doing it. For example, an interior designer may have gone into a firm as an assistant designer, but was involved principally in project management.

That experience may have involved contact with certain types of contractors or clients, and that may be very beneficial to a future project.

Is there experience in lighting? In acoustics? In any other type of specific design? What was really done on that job, and what were the accomplishments?

Consider the extra work that an employee has done, perhaps within a professional organization such as the American Society of Interior Designers (ASID), or the Institute of Business Designers (IBD). Did they gain experiences there? Did he or she hold an office, help run a convention, or organize an event? Has he or she done volunteer work that might develop certain talents?

What special abilities does this person have that might help the firm? It could be educational, such as knowing a foreign language or another discipline. It could be social: acquaintance with prospective clients. Or it could be a hobby.

For example, a designer I profiled in *Career Options for Designers* had learned stage design through his interest in the theater. He worked on two plays a year, and learned about lighting and stage presentation—skills he wouldn't have picked up in his practice. This background gave him an edge in creating outstanding lighting for many of his corporate jobs.

Page three asks for details of project experience: the type of project and when; the client or owner; the budget for the entire project. What was the budget for specific services rendered? What specific responsibilities did the staff person have, and what did he or she learn or accomplish on this project? After reviewing your staff, analyze the size of your firm and its general qualifications based on the staff members and all of their past experiences which we noted in our individual projects review.

A similar history is necessary for any consultants or associates who have gone into a joint venture with you. This should help you define what makes your firm unique.

SPECIALTIES

Among the more successful design firms of the seventies and eighties were those with high technical knowledge; they were able to say, "Here is a need and we are able to fill it." The market demands specialties, and this is part of the excitement of being in interior design today.

Originality pays, so look at your practice and see how you can work in more original elements. The smart thing to do is to try to design your program so that it's a little bit different and has a different label from any others. For example, everyone knows or can find out how what people charge per square foot for space planning. But if you can come up with a different name, such as "facility review work," then there is no direct way for the client to determine exactly how that compares to what your competitor offers.

You have the opportunity to develop a creative specialty that no one has considered. This makes me think that it is really wrong to take only one test to become an interior designer. I feel that you really need to be tested in each of the specialties. Obviously, if you specialized in law offices, you would need to understand their library requirements. If you are doing medical facilities, you must understand the codes and equipment that are required.

The specialty of residential design pays far better than any of the other design specialties. However, it takes a certain type of personality. You must be seen as a professional designer by your clients, who are therefore willing to give you the respect and freedom necessary to indulge in a high level of creativity, and earn the high income. The other area that pays very well is any specialty with a high degree of originality—something that no one else knows how to do, something very special.

Although one of the most lucrative specialties, residential design has been looked down on as too common and undistinguished. The feeling was that anyone with minimal training could do it. In reality, some of the most creative aspects of our discipline are in residential design. You can be more creative in a residential project because you really don't have to meet all the codes and technical requirements that commercial projects may require.

The next most profitable specialty is any project which demands a high level of creativity. When you offer goods or services that people have never seen before, the perceived value is higher. Can you do something unexpected, something highly inventive? When you design a project using only items from catalogs, anyone can buy that item. They can go to High Point, they can use an 800 number. But, if you specify an unusual finish or some other change that makes the product unique, then they are unlikely to question your pricing. So use your design ability to create that "something special."

You can choose from an extensive range of specialties. There are hundreds of specialties today, and every time I visit a new group I hear of a new specialty. Right now my list is almost 30 pages taken from *The Interior Design Business Handbook*. To date, they are:

> acoustic design
> airplane design
> apartment/condominium/co-op design
> aquarium design
> art dealing

audiovisual center design
barrier-free design for the physically limited
bathroom design
beauty and barber shop design
CADD specialist
ceramic tile design
code safety design law specialist
color consultation
commercial design
construction supervision
corporate campus design
corporate in-house design
country club design
design for children
design for in-home medical care
display/exhibit design
energy conservation design
ergonomic design
facility management
health club design
factory/production consulting
forensic consulting
mortuary design
furniture design
graphic design/signage
greenhouse design
hard surface flooring design
hardware design
health club design
historic preservation and adaptive re-use
hospitality design
interior landscaping
kennel design

kitchen design
journalism
legal office design
library design
licensing
lighting design
lighting fixture design
manufacturer's representative
marine design
marketing specialist
medical center design
medical office design
modular pre-fabricated design
mural painting
office art design
park design
party and ball design
photographic set design
plumbing fixture design
prison design
product design, evaluation and marketing
project management
psychiatric care facility design
public relations
purchasing
real estate development
rendering
residential design
restaurant design
restaurant kitchen design
retail and specialty selling
retail store design
security systems design

set design
shop-at-home services
shopping mall design
showroom design
solar design
stadium and arena design
storage design
tabletop display design
teleconference center design
tenant development services
textile design
training center design
transportation center design
turnkey services
real estate upgrading
vacation home design
wallcovering design
wall finishes
window treatment design

To gain the competitive edge, you need to try to present a slightly different product—something different from what everyone else is offering within your community, but not too different, because it's very difficult to make a profit being a missionary.

EXPERIENCE

Keeping a design project analysis on each and every job you do will give you a yardstick of past accomplishments for use in evaluating which potential projects are right for your firm. A sample form is included in this chapter to simplify the task. Reviewing your last five years of work will tell you what is easiest and most profitable for you. It also will help you pinpoint the type of work that your firm has done, as well as the work experience of your staff. These are important factors since you are offering principally service. The abilities of your team—yourself, your staff and consultants—are your product. Anyone can buy furnishings. It is the way you use them that makes your firm different from others.

This background is necessary to establish your marketing program, as well to price your projects. The effort you spend reviewing this will be useful throughout your practice. Analyze projects done four, five, six, and even ten years ago. Projects performed more than ten years ago have limited use for today's market although they should be considered.

Compare the abilities and skills of your staff then with those of your present staff; compare those past sources with those available today.

Determine which types of jobs have been most profitable for you in the past five years, and which can help you acquire the jobs you want in the next five years. A marketing structure must be based on work that is yet to be done, while building on the experience of past efforts. Of course it is best to analyze the projects when they are underway; trying to remember all the details three or four years later doesn't work.

Whether you use our form or not, your design project analysis should contain this basic information: client, size of project, whether you purchased or re-used furniture, the profit, and how you won the job.

THE DESIGN PROJECT ANALYSIS FORM

First, identify the client, address and phone number, along with the name of the contact person. What did you commonly call the project? Was it the name of the site, the building, the corporation or the client? Who worked on the project, what date was it begun and when did it end?

How large was the project? The analysis should tell you whether it was a new project, or whether it was remodeling; whether you were responsible for any interior architectural changes or recommendations; whether other architects and engineers and designers were involved. Depending on the size of your firm, you may want to define specific areas of carpeting, wall surface materials, drapery and window covering, and so on. Outline all the services your firm provided, from the basic design to follow-through with construction inspectors and feasibility studies, to presenting drawings.

Did you reuse pieces the client already owned, or were all new furnishings and equipment and finishes used? How much restoration was carried out on the building; what were the other changes? Was any of the furniture purchased through your company or your suggested vehicles, or did the client handle purchasing?

At the end of the project, when you evaluated the hours versus the income base, and your hourly fees versus the amount of profit, what was the profit? What was the final billing for professional service fees and purchases? How did that job look from an accountant's viewpoint, and how did it look from a design viewpoint? Did you accomplish what you wanted, or was it a project where, for any number of reasons, things didn't turn out quite the way you had expected.

What did the client think of the project when it was finally installed? Check to see what they think of it in three months, six months, a year, and perhaps two years. Also, check how the project has held up over that period of time.

Where did the job come from? Was the client a referral from an existing client, or a prospect brought in by your advertisements or public relations efforts? It is important to identify the source of the job so that additional marketing information can evolve. Include any factors that you feel contributed to your firm's being awarded the job.

Can you expect referrals from this project?

Finally, is there a potential for publicity on this job? After the project is complete, you may want to ask whether the client would enjoy or consider exposure in a magazine or publication.

When you have answered these questions concerning your projects of the past five years, analyze the projects by years. How many projects did you undertake in a year? What types were they, and how successful? What were the costs and percentages of profit for each job? This analysis should help you understand the trends of your company.

Obviously you want to identify which jobs have been profitable. However, even experience gained on projects that were unprofitable can be helpful in giving your firm the new direction that is often necessary to make it competitive in the present market.

Although your revenue base may change, it is advisable when reviewing the past projects to evaluate the income resources as they compare to the investments made in terms of time expended, marketing costs, and wear and tear on your firm.

PRODUCT

What is your product? With your firm's particular capabilities, what can you produce? There is no better way to ruin a design firm than by offering something that you cannot produce, a project that calls for abilities your firm lacks.

What is your best product? What can you do that is different from anyone else? In this instance, you want to look at not just the product, but also the quality of the product and services you offer. Do you specify for hospitals and institutions, or does your work entail very fine decorative detailing that is appropriate for only executive offices or fine residences? Do you design and specify or provide turnkey projects?

Identify the type of business most profitable and most appropriate for your firm. That is your best product. The clients who provide this work are your primary market.

A good product is one that can meet the wants and needs of clients, your capabilities, and the resources available. Does your service or product have a purpose that is viable today? Can you produce it within the confines of available human and material resources? Can you produce it within the time constraints and financial restrictions of the prospective client?

What size is your firm? Are you a one-, two- or three-person firm, or are you a hundred-person firm? Obviously, the types of projects you want to pursue are different in each situation. Still, it is becoming more common for small firms that coordinate, team or set up a joint venture with other groups to accomplish large projects. Many corporations find this type of joint venture very attractive. So, with the right structure, small firms are able to compete with large firms.

Can you define your product, and do so in a sentence? If someone at a party asks what type of work you do, you want to be able to set yourself apart from every other designer in the field. Are you able to explain your work in simple terms to someone who does not know our field, so that they could explain it to one of their friends or associates?

This is a big question, and one most of us can't answer without preparation.

How do you work? What is your preferred method? Our professional associations suggest that designers do no processing, sales or production; that we do merely design. According to professional design associations, designers should only work on a professional fee basis. These associations don't believe we should be in the business of selling merchandise because it's not truly professional. They also warn of the responsibilities and liabilities involved in selling merchandise; it is a specialized business that requires a completely different structure.

But design only will not work for all projects because you'll never be able to achieve the quality level you need with a design-only operation. Projects involving standard products can be specified and installed by any successful bidder. It would cost more to write the specifications for some specialized creative one-of-a-kind projects than to build the job. In some highly creative areas of design there are special techniques, even secret proprietary processes that may be essential to the design. A fabric design can be printed by almost any firm as long as they have the right ground cloth and screens, but the printing processes of Fortuny fabrics are too unusual. This proprietary process has kept the company in a strong position for generations.

If your work is highly creative and calls for a design-build situation, do you have what you need to complete this project? You may need to structure your own workroom, or create an exclusive joint venture or partnership with the appropriate craftspeople. Remember, ten percent of any project is design; the other ninety percent is making it happen. How is the project going to happen? Are you going to control it or will someone else take control?

Our clients want the extraordinary and there is an opportunity for high income—if a designer knows how to execute a project successfully. Therefore, special control is necessary. There are many special design processes that cannot be specified for mass production. They are handcrafted processes, tricks of the trade.

SALES FORCE

Sales is a highly skilled and organized profession, dedicated to bringing a needed product to a buyer—an interested person who can afford to buy our product. The design product can vary substantially, depending on the firm's specialty and the extent of services offered. The history and definition formulated under this profile will help determine the best method and salespersons to make up the force.

Today, the persons able to bring in sales are *most* often the highest earners within *most* firms; they usually dictate the direction of the job. Many firms will not employ anyone who does not bring in work and even the lowest level of support staff are expected to be out there generating business.

The position of a salesperson in a design firm has not always been respected. In fact, the marketing or sales department often occupied the last office down the hall. Today, the CEO or other top executive of most leading firms is a marketing or salesperson. Very often a sales or marketing position is the highest paid position within a design firm. The salesperson determines the direction and the success of the firm. After all, if we don't have work, we can't design.

Some designers don't like to sell. If this is the case, then team up with a partner who *lives* to sell. To succeed at selling, you must enjoy the process or you won't be willing to go the extra mile necessary to win the job.

To determine who should be handling the sales, first define exactly what product you are presenting and to what types of clients. Reexamine your past projects to enable you to pin down a past client profile, your product, and a profile of potential clients before you decide upon the appropriate sales force. You may have to define other parts of your marketing plan and then come back to this section.

Consider what is most comfortable for you, but be aware that your marketing plan requires a sales force. Once you find the contacts and know where you're going, you will need to consider who will carry out the next part of your marketing effort.

Make a list of everyone within your firm. Each person should play some position on your sales force or marketing team. Review the individual abilities of each employee and the areas in which they would have some outside involvement.

Do you work with another company or design professional whose product or service complements yours? Perhaps you can create a specialized market together that you could not have accomplished alone. Often two small offices can team together, or engage in a joint venture in order to compete successfully with much larger firms. Look for a simple way to merge with the goal of supplying the extraordinary, that unique service that can put you in a non-competitive market.

INCOME PROFILE

Using information from the Design Project Analysis form you filled out for projects of the past five years, review your methods of charging, profit, and percentage of profit on each project. This should provide you with a clear understanding of where your past revenues came from.

Compare the project profiles to the profit results. What kinds of projects were most profitable for you? Designers tend to think of the project or client they liked the best as the most profitable, but you may find that "ordinary" projects earned you the greatest profit.

Profit bases change. The moneymaker of yesterday or today may not be viable tomorrow, so compare your history with the current market. That specialty of yours that brought in higher revenues may now be a common practice that everyone else provides at lower fees.

At one time space planning was a highly paid specialty. Today there are computer programs designed for space planning. Every client knows the cost per square foot for a specific type of plan. Design firms must develop new services on which to base their incomes.

(There is more information on selling in the second part of this book.)

Design Staff Questionnaire

Name: _____ Address: _____ Phone No.: _____

_____ Date: _____

Education:

Design School or College: | Accomplishments:

Dates: From: | To:

Degree Received:

Courses Studied:		From:	To:

Awards Received:	What was done to earn this award?

Other Education: (workshops, seminars, etc.)		
Subject:	Accomplishments:	Dates Attended:

© *Design Business Monthly*

Figure 4-1a

Design Staff Questionnaire

Employment Experience: _____

Company: _____ From: _____ To: _____

Your Title: _____

Job Experience: _____

Accomplishments: _____

Company: _____ From: _____ To: _____

Your Title: _____

Job Experience: _____

Accomplishments: _____

Company: _____ From: _____ To: _____

Your Title: _____

Job Experience: _____

Accomplishments: _____

Company: _____ From: _____ To: _____

Your Title: _____

Job Experience: _____

Accomplishments: _____

Professional organizations to which you belong and offices, committees or posts that you have held in these organizations:

Organization: Accomplishments:

Any special abilities or knowledge that you feel would be of benefit to the firm, ie: certain social acquaintances, fluency in foreign languages, knowledge within other disciplines, list of prospective clients with whom you are familiar or have had experience:

Experience: Accomplishments:

Figure 4-1b

Design Staff Questionnaire

Design Project Experience:

Type: Date:

Client or Owner:

Cost of Total Project:

Cost of Work Done by Design Firm:

Services Rendered by Design Firm:

Your Responsibilities:

Accomplishments on this Project:

Type: Date:

Client or Owner:

Cost of Total Project:

Cost of Work Done by Design Firm:

Services Rendered by Design Firm:

Your Responsibilities:

Accomplishments on this Project:

Other Relative Information:

Page 3

Figure 4-1c

Design Project Analysis

Client: _____ Project: _____ Staff: _____

Address: _____ Contact: _____ Date: _____ Started: _____

Phone: _____ Completed: _____

Type of Construction: (new, renovation, etc.)

Size of Project:

Construction Budget:

Furnishings Budget:

Type of Services the Firm Provided:

Design Accomplishments:

Size of the Fee:

Source of the Job:

Method of Charging:

Expected Referrals:

Profit of the Project:

Percentage of Profit on Total Project:

Figure 4-2

Chapter 5

The Marketplace

In the 1990s, if you're putting all of your time into new business development every month, you're in trouble. You will be spending too much time and money to build a successful practice. Now is the time to develop existing clients and keep them happy, while creating a bank of prospective clients. People purchase design services because of need. That need may not be specific or concrete; it may be psychological. Identifying the needs and aspirations of our clients is market research.

Some of this is part of day-to-day practice, where we collect client responses to various interactions and general trends. The more time you spend up front listening to what clients want, defining their needs and their projects, the easier it is to design and produce the project. Good research increases your chances of a successful project, one that is based on understanding and good rapport, and that will bring you referrals for new clients.

The marketplace of the nineties demands that we be proactive as opposed to reactive. We must seek out the clients and use polished methods to develop the job. Don't wait until a client asks you for direction, but investigate a client's need and design programs to meet those potential needs.

Successful design firms find ways to meet potential clients before a formal request for proposal is issued. They don't wait to be put in the position of competing with other design companies. Instead, they establish relationships with potential clients by reviewing their client list and by continuing rapport with past clients.

To succeed, we must investigate and seize any kind of opportunity to become part of a client's team. As design professionals, we cannot afford to be seen as marketers and sellers, but need to be regarded as people who understand the client's need, and who will function as teammates to solve that problem.

SERVICE

This next decade is a service period. Design firms, in fact almost all industries, will be dedicated to servicing clients. This is a cause for concern: our clients think of the furnishings field as providing a tremendous amount of service, based on its past tradition. Years ago, it was traditional for furniture stores to take care of your parents for years on end. If there was a problem with the furniture, even five years after it was purchased, your parents called the store, which sent a person to repair it. Furniture stores then worked on a keystone mark-up. They had a profit range that allowed them to provide these services.

Today, especially in the design field, firms are working on a very small spread of four to twelve percent. Providing continuing care is expensive and not possible on this margin. This is something we need to review before positioning ourselves with our clients.

Although clients today expect and demand customer service, the basics of customer service are not part of the standard design curriculum, and many design firms are ill-prepared to meet the ongoing demands of the client.

Today clients don't want just a beautiful design, great presentation and beautiful boards: they expect a job to be completed for a certain budget within a specified amount of time. Why? In many past instances, clients paid a tremendous amount of money for design and the bids they received for the project were for three or four times the amount of money available. As a result, we now see managers of community projects and corporate projects going out on bids with cost ceilings, and saying, "We have 35 million dollars to do this project; please give us a proposal to design, to build and to complete the project within this range." This is what the client wants to buy.

How do interior design firms fit into this? In order to be considered for this type of project, a firm must form a partnership or a joint venture with all the necessary design specialists, architects, engineers, landscape architects, vendors, and contractors. We must design the project so that it can be completed within the restrictions of the job.

Talk to your clients. Some of them just want a beautiful and wonderful project, and they're willing to pay for this. Other clients need a product that works, that's productive. Just as a factory produces, so most our studios. We must be willing to look at a client's financial statements and to tell the client, "It is only appropriate for you to spend a certain amount of money on your office in this period." Then you have to decide what can be done within that budget to meet the client's needs, and whether you can work within that range.

This is the trend for the way jobs are going to be built. We have to be part of a client's corporation, a member of the team. We can't just sit across the table advising them; we have to develop a program with that corporation.

CLIENT PROFILE

Who are your current clients? What do they have in common, and what are their differences? Look through your Design Project Analysis forms to refresh your memory and develop a profile of your current client.

Consider common attitudes about buying interior design services: what your clients liked best about the experience and what they liked least.

WHAT ARE CUSTOMERS LOOKING FOR?

1. They are looking for professional assistance. They come to the designer because they want to accomplish their project at a higher skill level than they are capable of doing.
2. They want you to see them as a very special and important person. They believe that they should be first in your practice and it is up to your firm to treat them this way.
3. They want to reduce their doubt. They don't know much about this field and they know there will be many decisions to make. With your input, they will have more confidence in their decisions.
4. They want a designer who they believe respects them, listens to them, and understands them. If you are not willing to exert the energy to really listen to your clients and to take the trouble to be sure that you understand what they want as well as their reasons for wanting it, then find yourself another client. Some personalities just don't work well together.
5. They come to you because they have a project which is beyond their capabilities and they want you to assist them in

making it happen. They want you to take some of the problems away and show them that these problems can be solved with professionalism.

THE MATURE MARKET

America today is called "the greying society." This means that there will soon be more people over sixty years of age than there are under twenty years of age—something our country has never seen before. This former group has discretionary income and is psychologically prepared and interested in its interior environments.

These people in their sixties form a discriminating market. They know what they want and they know exactly what they want to buy. They are well educated, not just in terms of where they went to school, but in terms of life experience. They have invested time in reading about and studying the design items they want to add to their living environments.

They may have physical limitations brought on by aging, so the interiors must be easy to use. They want comfortable, workable, attractive spaces.

They expect active customer service. These people want things done for them, and need a design practice that is staffed to service their needs now, not next week or next month.

It is a growth market, but study it to determine whether it's the right one for your combination of skills, goals and experience. It demands special attention to communication. There are marketing specialists who dedicate their careers to these issues.

Finally, if you are planning an advertisement to appeal to the mature market, make sure that the type size is large enough to be read easily. Presbyopia (farsightedness) is common among the after-60 set.

DEVELOPING YOUR LIST OF POTENTIAL CLIENTS

Who needs what we have to offer? Not everyone needs or wants it, and if they don't want it, we'd better find another client. So the question is, who is looking for our services? Who is making major changes?

What is the potential? You may find that if your firm's direction has changed, you need to add different clients. Based on your company's abilities, who should you be looking for?

Your prospective client list starts with the Design Project Analysis forms filled out to review past work and accomplishments to help you define your company profile. Reviewing the Design Project Analysis gives you references, profiles of past customers, and a list of contacts for potential work. This list is the basis for maintaining a rapport with existing clients and is a good base for developing and maintaining a good marketing program.

Existing market trends must be considered. Even if your past projects are not exactly the types of projects available and in demand at present, reviewing them will give us some basis for building our preferred group of prospects.

This is where research comes in. You must narrow the field of potential clients to those you can reasonably expect to reach. For instance, not everyone in your city wants or can afford design services. Of those who want design services, some want skills outside your experience. Can those who want design services afford them? There are many ways to find the answers. Run credit reports. Talk to other professionals. Identify the potential clients and their needs. Refining your definition of potential clients gives you a better chance of reaching them.

Then build a sales program around that particular type of client. From that point on, your program may consist of a series of letters, phone calls or invitations to various seminars or programs, or an on-going list of activities that builds the program.

REFERRALS

Prospects are often based on referrals. Interior design is a sizeable investment. Most prospective clients are wary of hiring a designer of whom they know nothing. If a firm's work is good, a large percentage of their work will come in by referrals. Anyone who uses an interior designer creates a demand among his or her friends and acquaintances for design work.

Obtaining work through referrals should not be a random process. Many companies whose work is mostly through referrals have an organized program. Do set aside a regular contact time for talking to past clients in order to learn about potential jobs. You're unlikely to get referrals just by sitting and waiting for them. You will have to dig and move and work with your referrals to develop them into paying clients. Everything is subject to change: the economy, your practice, your clients' practices. Does their new direction fit with what you are doing?

Some people work well with friends, and others prefer an arms-length relationship. You alone can decide whether you want to work with friends. Still, many designers began their careers in this way.

Ask your staff members if they know people who might be influential in buying or directing a building or furnishing project. Ask them to consider college roommates, friends, neighbors, relatives, landlords, past employers, or people who serve on the board of directors of a firm or organization. Hold regular meetings to update this list. Keep your staff thinking about who they know, and ask them to gather as much information as they can about these people.

Other good sources for referrals are other professionals—architects, engineers, other designers. Check into what they're doing.

Interview both general contractors and subcontractors to learn the types of projects in which they are involved and if there is a need for a design professional. Your contractors can be one of your most important marketing tools. They are often able to develop and to direct work to your firm. The closer you work with a contractor, and the more mutual respect you develop, the better chance you stand of getting good referrals.

In an economy where budgets are so very tight, the interior designers and architects who form a very close relationship with their contractors are often able to save money during a project. The contractors might suggest cost-cutting measures and let the designers decide whether these measures would compromise design. This interaction has proved beneficial in so many ways that design firms have incorporated it into their working styles. Including your contractors in your project and using them as consultants before detailing the final job, can ensure that you both understand all the construction parameters of the project. When there is a wide range of costs in a project put out to bid, it invariably means that the prints are not well documented and there is room to change orders and problems. If your prints and documents are so well-detailed that all the contractors understand them, the potential for problems is much less.

Manufacturers, representatives, wholesalers, suppliers, and distributors all have salespeople in the field and are often aware of future projects. They know the type of furniture we buy, the types of products we buy, and which jobs we do best. They've seen some of our finished projects and they feel part of our firm.

• REFERRALS •

Make an on-going file of potential referrals:

Childhood friends

    Neighborhood

    Elementary School

    High School

    College

    Other Seminars

    Other Causes

Family Friends

    Yours

    Your parents'

    Your sisters' and brothers'

    Spouse

    Children

Community Activities

    Clubs, country or social

    Special interests

    Church

    Charities

    Past employment

Business Associates

    Other professionals

    Vendors

    Contractors

Review each client similarly. The more you know about your clients, the easier it is to put them into a profile and find similar sources for referrals.

You can easily list three or more people within each area.

OUR RESOURCES

What supplies, trades and craftspeople are available to us? Sometimes clients want items we simply cannot obtain. Before setting your marketing direction, be sure you have the backup resources to fill the needs of your design. If your specialty demands that everything be individually crafted, you must control or at least be very close to an excellent shop.

To produce good design, we must use great products. We also need to know the resource firms and their abilities. These firms change often. Many of those that were prominent a few years ago are not around any longer; many new companies are springing up.

A close relationship between vendors and designers would make our access to new technical information more timely. Our sources are a great source of technical information. Timely information means the right product will be specified for the right places.

Build a close relationship with consultants and suppliers and learn to know them well. Also, we must let them know when products don't perform appropriately. How else will they know whether the product measures up? We are part of their quality control system.

This way we can deliver the highest quality finished product at the most effective price. In this tight economy, we have neither the time nor financial resources to build new relationships on each new project. We need to have our working teams ready at all times.

COMPETITION

Look at the movers and the shakers in your field and see how
they're handling their marketing. You may be doing things
better than they are, but perhaps they have a different method
of presenting their abilities.

Questions to answer about your competition:

1. Who are they?
2. Who are the most important?
3. What kind of staff do they have?
4. Who are their clients?
5. What is their marketing plan?
6. What services do they provide?
7. What is their direction?
8. How do they charge?
9. What are their successes?
10. What are their problems?
11. What can we learn from them?

Who makes the best income in interior design today?
Interior designers face stiff competition. Interior design services can be purchased at almost any corner, from the office
supply store, the specialty furniture shop, through the mail,
or by phone. This fierce competition has fostered rivalry
among design disciplines that used to work together. Architects, engineers, and other design professionals now offer
interior design services because they believe it is possible to
charge more for some of these services. They believe this so
firmly that in some states, legislation has been successfully
introduced that prohibits anyone other than architects from
doing types of work that have traditionally been the province
of interior designers.

What many people often do not realize is that interior design as practiced by interior designers is more detailed than interior design by architects. We put a lot more effort into a project for our dollars or per square foot than do architects. Their dollar budgets are considerably larger and a lot less detailed. There are some areas where perhaps clients don't need equal services, and so these variables come into play.

The reason that it is so important that we know about our competition is that we are making the assumption that design firms have limited amounts of money to spend either in marketing or on sales overhead. It is important to be able to spend that money effectively. Consider the cost of running your firm; how much markup do you need to cover your expenses? Example: If your firm is running on a 30 to 35 percent mark-up requirement, there is no point in competing with people who are doing similar work, or work which our clients may see as similar, using only a five or ten percent mark-up. Such an approach will be generally fruitless. Therefore, if we must compete with them we should offer either a different way of doing things and a different way of presenting a project—or we must go to different clients. Now you can see why time spent learning as much as you can about your competitors is extremely beneficial and necessary: it saves you a lot of effort. Sometimes the highly publicized jobs everyone is competing prove to be the least profitable, because by the time so much competition is involved, there is almost no profit left for anyone. Very often the little jobs will pay so much better because they are unknown and offer you an opportunity to do the very specialized things at which you excel, and to use your design creativity—rather than simply bidding on a job that is based purely on the lowest bidder.

LOCATION

What geographic limitations should you set for the type of work you want to attract? For example: Some types of work, such as residential or detailed contract work, are better located close by so that you can visit the site often in order to avoid most problems. Because the project is small, it could cost more to write the specifications than to build the project.

Larger projects usually are based on documentation and specifications, and the project management is carried out by others. If you know your specialty and its requirements, it's really no problem—you can work perhaps globally.

What is the type of design work that you are going to manage? Look at this first, and then establish your geographic limitations.

We found in our own practice that on highly creative work, we perform better when projects are closer to home. Therefore, we will only consult on distant projects. When the project demands hands-on project management, we want it close so that we can visit the site and manage the project as we feel it should be managed.

FACTORS THAT AFFECT OUR MARKETPLACE

A tight economy is a red flag warning that change may be needed in the way interior designers market their services. There are many potential clients who want our services, but are they able and willing to pay? As you select your specialty and develop a marketing approach, keep in mind that you need to be sure that those who want your services can afford to pay for them.

Business and economic conditions cause change. Change is part of interior design. I think it is necessary for designers to keep track of changing business trends, otherwise we might be doing business as usual while the market disappears. Keep track of business changes and incorporate them into the way you practice design. You'll find a list of sources for information on trends in the section on market research.

SOCIAL AND CULTURAL

Social and cultural concerns also affect business. *Interior Design* magazine recently dedicated an entire issue to environmental concerns, an indication that more and more design firms and their clients are concerned with ecology.

Accessibility is both a social concern and a legal issue. The Americans with Disabilities Act calls for new buildings to be barrier-free.

REGULATORY FORCES

Government, legal and regulatory forces affect our ability to work. Sometimes the number of laws and liabilities is so great that I'm afraid to work in a certain market. Look at these issues. Understand what it will cost you to do business and what laws affect your practice. For instance, in some states laws are written to limit the practice of interior design to architects. Interior designers still practice in those states, but it means that they have no legal recourse in the case of a dispute with a client.

TECHNOLOGY

Changing technology can affect our businesses overnight. For instance, the personal computer changed not just the business environment, but the personal environment. It is possible to purchase furniture and services via computer, and this was unheard of a few years ago. People can work at home part of the week, keeping in touch with their office by computer linkups. This may mean businesses need less desk space, as employees who work at home and in the office can share office space. But it also means that residential clients need professional space in their homes.

Some fields work well with off-site contributors. Other industries have come to realize the advantage of planned environments. People work better in surroundings that support their individual activities.

Video catalogs are available from several manufacturers; some design firms use video portfolios. Computer-assisted drawing (CAD) programs are no longer the wave of the future, but a necessity in some design specialties. CAD-users say it takes no less time to create a drawing on computer, but the ability to make almost instantaneous changes is invaluable.

Computers are used to assure accuracy in highly creative design work. In addition to the production phase of design, they have become a part of marketing and selling processes by encouraging customization. The client makes selections from a computerized menu.

The concept of mass-customizing is explained in Stanley M. David's *Future Perfect* (Addison Wesley Publishing, Reading, Mass., 1987, page 158). In the Japanese housing industry, mass-produced factory-built homes are constructed to the buyer's individual design. The buyer works with the sales representative and can select from among twenty thousand components as well as lay out the details of the home on a computer screen. Several hours later, the buyer has a customized plan.

Finished plans are sent electronically to the factory and produced on an assembly line one-third of a mile long. In thirty to sixty days, the custom two- or three- bedroom house is totally finished, including wiring and final details, and is delivered to the buyer's site.

Using modern technology in every step of the design and building process—from the computer catalog of parts, to the drafting of the plan, to the controlled production line for building—housing manufacturers can provide extensively customized detail at an effective price.

The major manufacturer of prefab manufactured homes in Japan makes 110,000 units per year. In the United States, the largest manufacturer of similar units produces only two thousand per year.

Mass-customizing on a different scale is practiced by the paint supplier Benjamin Moore & Co., which delivers true colors that match precisely the samples for its extensive color line. The firm provides its dealers with computers that measure light frequencies of color samples. This computerized control permits a perfect color match every time the store mixes a batch of paint. Even an amateur can produce perfectly matched colors.

Everywhere we look, the computer is changing American industry. This valuable tool was only a dream ten years ago.

Chapter 6

Market Research

Market research can help interior design businesses stay successful during a downturn in the economy, suggests a publication by the Institute of Business Designers (funded by Polsky/Fixtures Furniture Endowment with a grant from Joe Polsky). The guide, *A Survival Report*, examines how eleven design businesses in Texas handled the disastrous decline in business following the 1980 petrochemical crisis and the resulting economic disaster for Texas.

The design businesses observed for the report found that the first issue was how much work needed to be done; cost was second; then came design. It wasn't a question of whether the design was beautiful. Interior designers had to research very heavily into the reasons for purchasing design. They learned that you can never know too much about your potential clients. This period in the 1980s brought the designers much closer to their existing clients and made them realize that as designers, they must offer a very high quality, well-priced project.

Many of the firms have survived, but learned that in the contract field there is not much loyalty from clients.

Selecting a design firm was done on a single-project basis. That meant that the cost of marketing and developing that project became a more important factor. There is not much point in accepting a job on which you will lose money if it won't generate repeat business. Having to justify the cost of marketing changed the way design firms bid projects and the way they worked.

The results were that designers had to spend considerable amounts of time developing clients and finding new ones.

For the design firms examined in the report, the final decision for the majority of new jobs depended on the facilities manager. Here was a different kind of client, more sophisticated and closely involved in controlling the design process from the financial viewpoint. Time and budget issues became a major part of the reason why one firm was selected over another. The design firms that won the projects offered a high level of service and were responsible for controlling the projects' finances.

Some firms decided to diversify geographically, extending their services to parts of the country which were hit less hard. (At this point, many of the surviving firms are not just national, but international.) Most of the design firms covered by the report reviewed their client base to identify specific design needs and how these could be met. They also looked for joint ventures with other companies, developing the kinds of relationships that allowed them to apply their expertise on pre-existing projects outside their normal geographic area for marketing.

They realized that specialization was important, but that it had to be on a national basis; their market areas had to grow much wider. To maintain their specialties rather than taking any project that came along, many of them opened new offices in other market areas. This entailed extensive traveling, which could be exhausting and expensive. It also meant investing in electronic linkages via computer, fax and telephone, to enable them to contact their vendors and consultants all around the country more quickly. Fortunately, the technology existed to meet their needs.

Design firms have learned that to stay profitable in slow times, they must focus on clients' needs and wants. This is not a time to entice or educate, but to expend effort to find out what potential clients believe they need and design our presentation accordingly. This effort builds rapport, putting the design team in the position of friend or team member. Responding to a perceived need is part of an understanding relationship built on mutual respect. Do everything you can to encourage your clients to see your relationship as dedicated to their best interests.

A downturn in the economy is the time to step up your advertising and promotion, even though your budget may be short. Use some of your creativity to develop a program that enhances your image and keeps your firm's name before your prospective clients.

THE BASICS

Market research is an important tool for the design firm, as we are dealing with such a specific market. Market research identifies the client, their backgrounds and their needs. It gives you your market segment, a subgroup of the entire population. Positioning, the image a company projects with respect to its customers and competition, is one step of a marketing plan.

In the 1960s there was a strong emphasis on focus group research. Marketers would bring a group of people together to get their response to a specific product or offering. The response then became the basis for approaching other clients. Focus group research has been valuable in determining just how a product is accepted by a specific group.

In the 1970s marketers coined the term 'psychographics,' which in essence means that people with similar lifestyles and similar habits respond in similar ways. Marketers in the 1980s combined psychographics with computers to amass and collate large amounts of data quickly. In the nineties leading marketers are already developing different ways of identifying consumer needs and stimulating buying.

You can hire someone to do this for you, but few design firms are large enough to afford the luxury. If you can afford it and want a professional market researcher, a good place to start is with *Bradford's Directory of Marketing Research Agencies*, 50 Argyle Ave., New Rochelle, New York. It lists firms, their principals, number of employees, and the types of marketing research they undertake.

A good market research professional, someone who dedicates his or her energies to the field, probably has a proven track record. A person who does nothing but market research may be more skilled at it than an advertising agency or public relations firm would be.

Is it expensive? Yes it is, but sometimes spending three or four thousand dollars could save you time and money. In fact, a firm that spent four thousand on a research project saved $150,000: it had allotted that amount to a strong program but found it would not be well-received, and ultimately did not undertake the program. Even if you're doing small programs, test small market groups, talk to your clients, stay in touch, and keep a record of the results. Don't collect information for its own sake; collect information you can use.

TOOLS OF MARKET RESEARCH

Where can we obtain information, what type of information do we need and where are we to go for this information? Newspapers, business publications, magazines and state-wide organizations are source material for the research marketer. Special-interest publications such as the *Wall Street Journal*, *Barron's*, *Business Week*, *Forbes*, *Time*, *The New York Times*, and others help you spot the trends. They report on what companies are doing and the changes they are making.

The U.S. government is the largest publisher in the world; you can make good use of government publications if you know how to find them. A popular guide is available by writing to the U.S. Superintendent of Documents, Government Printing Office, Washington, DC 20402. You can request catalogs and specific recommendations for publications in this way or contact the Small Business Administration Office or the Department of Commerce field offices.

McGraw-Hill publishes the *Dodge Reports*, which lists buildings under construction by geographic areas. Other data included are design firms involved, details of the contracts, and other professionals involved.

Standard & Poor's *Industrial Surveys* analyzes trends in construction utilities and transportation.

Local papers published by statewide business organizations can be valuable. And don't underestimate the value of local newspapers and magazines!

Which section should you check first in your local newspaper? You may want to look at the sections on companies on the move, and on changes within the community. On a daily basis, look at firms that are hiring. Look at firms that are looking for new types of personnel, because if they're changing their personnel, they are likely to be changing their interior spaces, and they will need design services.

SOURCES FOR TRENDS

Learn to look for and recognize the trends. Before you can create a marketing plan, you need to investigate what is happening in the interior design field now and in the next twelve months. We are in a dramatically service-oriented period, a period where even the design superstars must work harder on marketing. Most new projects are being awarded to people who handle a need, firms that understand clients and are willing to be part of their team—design firms which, like Nordstroms department stores, go just a bit further to ensure customer satisfaction. This means that it takes a different type of presentation and a different type of staffing. Your firm's organization, business programs and structures must be devised with this type of client in mind.

Real estate agents and building owners know when companies are on the move or purchasing properties. Cultivate a source in the real estate field. Some firms have developed great practices just because they know one or two strong people in the real estate field. Owners of any large project, such as an apartment building or office building, are a good source of information on new tenants. Usually these owners want to set and maintain a design standard and tone for their building, and are therefore happy to share this information. Every region has several organizations dedicated to business development. The Chamber of Commerce is one of many. Some organizations handle business development for very specialized groups, such as minority-owned firms.

Often community government officials are aware of new building projects and industries coming into your area. Keeping in touch with your local officials gives you an early warning of local trends.

The government is a major purchaser of design services and products today. It is a special type of client with specific communication requirements, both in qualifying a project and in documenting the job. To formulate the appropriate approach, you may want to attend a course on the subject. The Small Business Administration and/or other local business development organizations offer courses, as well as up-to-date guides and contact lists.

Chapter 7

Targeting the Right Clients

Now that you have defined your company through a company profile and examined the marketplace needs, compare your findings. How well do the skills and abilities your company has to offer fit the demands of the marketplace?

You have a general profile of potential clients. Now is the time to narrow it down to a definition of the best client you would like to attract. Do this by defining good and bad clients.

GOOD CLIENTS

1. Good clients see your firm as a partner and an asset.
2. They ask your firm to do work that is within the realm of what you do best.
3. They are demanding in a way that stimulates your staff to perform at its highest level.
4. Good clients respect and follow the directions you present as a result of mutual project development by your team and theirs.
5. Finally, good clients are willing to pay you appropriately for the energies and commitment you dedicate to their project.

BAD CLIENTS

1. Bad clients do not value your firm and are unwilling to develop or continue a relationship. They don't give you the time and information you need to develop the job.

2. Bad clients ask you to perform work that is outside your experience or specialty. They make demands for types of work that may be your weak points—you are not prepared to handle their day-to-day support or extensive paper flow, for example. Their style of management is drastically different from yours.

3. Bad clients do not follow your professional direction. After much design effort has been invested, the bad client will change the design and do it his or her own way without considering the problems this change will cause elsewhere.

4. Bad clients weaken you and your staff by decreasing your enjoyment in your work.

5. Finally, bad clients don't want to pay appropriately for the efforts you extend on their behalf.

Profitable firms build on the common denominator. Know who your best client is. Many designers believe their best clients are those whose projects they enjoyed working on, or those who are easy to get along with. But there are other factors to consider, such as comparing the time invested, the project budget, the profit, and any referrals you derived from the work.

In any good project, the client has to make demands. They must want to live and work in appropriate and well-designed spaces. Some may communicate these demands by calling you forty times a day; but being demanding doesn't necessarily mean being a pest. Good clients must feel that their spaces are important, or they will not be willing to invest the money, time and effort it takes to produce a good project.

A project can only be as good as the client. You relate better to clients when you understand their behavior, what they want or will do, when and how. Learn about this best client's behavior. Is the client's profession one that is steeped in tradition or one that is known for swift action?

Do they want budgets appropriate to their situations? The client's firms must show a profit, so there is an upset limit on what they can appropriately spend. If they underspend, the project will not meet the required standards for their need. If they overspend, it will overtax their finances. If a firm spends $100,000 on a building and its yearly income is only $200,000, a difference of $25,000 is monumental. To mortgage the client for the rest of his or her life to do design work on an office or an apartment is foolish. There must be a balance between the cost, the use, and the funds available.

What attitudes do the best clients have? They may be able to afford anything, but they just don't spend the money. How do they value design? Education and exposure are part of that best client's background. If they have never seen it, they probably don't want it.

What services must you provide? How much effort and expense will you incur to win the project? We can afford many things, but not everything.

We all like to think we are individuals, but we seem to fall into patterns. The more precisely a design firm can define its best client, the better it can serve them.

CHOOSING THE RIGHT JOBS

You must determine which clients are worth approaching and how much it seems wise to invest in each individual project.

Larger projects and continuing commissions are the most financially desirable projects, but keep in mind that there is a great deal of competition for those jobs. Sometimes the most lucrative projects come from smaller clients with whom your firm has a rapport. Review your success in getting jobs. If you are trying for projects in a certain geographic area and you've lost the last six or eight, you are either going after the wrong jobs or your marketing presentation needs to be rethought.

What kind of project do you do best? What do you do so well that you can do it without even thinking? There is usually one type of project that you know how to handle almost completely without any point of reference, any reviewing, any studying, or talking to anyone else. It is something that you know inside and out.

Define your best work. It should be the cornerstone of your marketing plan. There is no point in spending time, money and effort to win projects that are hard to produce and unprofitable.

When I look at a project, I estimate how much of it is familiar and easy for our firm to accomplish. If we are familiar with at least 70 or 80 percent of the project, I know that we can produce it with no problem. The minute you find this drops below 70 percent I suggest that you run from the job! Stay as far away from it as possible because there is far too much risk involved. Yes, I like a little creativity . . . but keep that creativity at no more than 30 percent and you'll safeguard your ability to manage and profit on the project.

A little challenge is great but don't let the challenges get too high. Sometimes a project seems too exciting to pass up. If you want a project that really doesn't relate to your past experiences, there are ways to team up and work with other people to develop the job. Still, you must take risk into account. If you involve other professionals, will the job then be profitable? How can you manage this project, keep your client happy and come home with a bit of profit at the end of the job? It all comes down to profitability.

The fastest way to ruin a company is to allow it to grow too fast or to take the wrong projects. What jobs are right for your firm? What jobs are most profitable? A project can involve dollar amounts and seem prestigious yet still be less profitable than most other work.

My firm worked on a country club project a few years ago, a highly visible project with active committees. At the same time we had another project that was simply replacing textiles. The two projects produced just about the same dollar volume. The textile replacement project was with a client with whom we had worked two or three times, and was completed very quickly. We did it in a matter of hours. We worked on the country club project for weeks and months on end, from six in the morning until eleven at night many days. Obviously, it was less profitable than the textile replacement project.

As you look at the profit on your projects versus the time you've spent, you come to realize which jobs are right for your firm. And it is best to look for jobs within that range. Some jobs may be financially beyond your abilities. Other projects may simply take too long. Or a fast-track job may come in at the wrong time for you.

Each time you consider a project, take into account these issues.

1. Is this the right job for your firm? Is it an area of design with which you are familiar?
2. Is it the right size?
3. Is there an opportunity for professional growth? Does the job offer new challenges? Otherwise it's not stimulating.
4. Can your client make decisions? Some people can't. One corporate firm that I know of has been working on a decision for nearly seven years, and they have yet to assign

the project. It just can't seem to make a decision within this area of work. So try to learn how well a firm makes decisions, or the job may never get off the ground.

5. Have you had past experience in working with a firm? Is there an established relationship?

6. What experience does the client have in working with designers?

7. Will you be working with reasonable people? Are they overly demanding and impossible? If they have been unreasonable with the contractors and other designers on the project, they're probably going to be the same with you.

8. Is the timing right? Will you have to rush to prepare your proposal? Usually, a poor proposal is worse than no proposal. Can you complete the job within the expected schedule? Does it fit into your current schedule? Has the client allowed adequate time to do the job properly?

9. Does the client pay his or her bills? Before you decide to take on a new client, obtain credit reports and check with other people they've worked with. If it will be impossible to collect your fees, it's better to stop right now!

10. Is the potential client connected to a competitor? Do they have a relative or a very close friend in the field who is also a designer, or has a furniture business, or a dealership? If so, it is probably not worth any great effort to pursue this client.

11. What is the competition? How many other firms are vying for the job?

12. What will it cost you to develop this client? We can go after almost any type of project, but some projects are more expensive than they are worth. Look at your cost in time and money, and decide if it's worth it.

13. Will this job be profitable?

Chapter 8

Techniques That Develop and Nurture Relationships

After you have established who you are going to develop—your new list of prospective clients—decide how you want to build a bridge between your firm and this "best" client. Because it takes five to ten contacts to develop a client, you may wish to use a combination of several techniques from this section.

A plan based on building bridges between the firm and the client can include many different techniques. These include public relations, promotional mailings, publicity, advertising, networking, entering design contests, entertaining, community service, and participating in show houses. If you have a message to bring to the public, you could try writing articles or public speaking. There are as many methods as there are designers. Some of the techniques that work for designers are presented here.

- Selecting methods compatible with your style of business.
- Choosing the staff person or persons best able to accomplish these goals.
- Allowing a budget for the tools needed to carry out your plan.
- Arranging your schedule to support the program.
- Commiting yourself.

PUBLIC RELATIONS

Public relations has three goals. It makes you known to your resources, your peers, and to your potential clients. Any public relations person you hire will tell you that those first two are easy enough to accomplish, but that the third one is much more difficult.

The success of a public relations program is reflected in the firm's ability to win business, or in the resulting sales. If you have targeted your market and developed a good definition of your firm's specialty, your chances for success are better.

There are two basic methods of obtaining sales. One is direct. The indirect method consists of creating a desire, which is part of marketing. This can be achieved by advertising, public relations, and other types of business development.

Advertising is a direct method of saying that you have something specific to sell. With advertising you take aim at your specific target audience. Direct mail allows the same control. Publicity, an aspect of public relations, is more indirect. You depend on a publicist or an editor to write appropriately about your firm.

In its broadest sense, public relations is any interaction between you or your representatives and your market. How do you sound when you answer the telephone? Each person on your staff who comes into contact with clients should present him or herself in a way that reflects well on your firm.

Public relations includes customer service, and doing the best job you can possibly do. Encourage clients to think of you as being part of their team. The hours and the energy that you spend working with those clients will be rewarded manyfold.

Keep in touch with your current clients. You should talk to your current clients on a weekly basis and your past clients preferably on a monthly or quarterly basis. This is one of your best sources of referrals.

WHERE DO YOU SPEND YOUR TIME?

The way we spend our time and where we spend our time can greatly contribute to our marketing efforts. Are you spending time where your potential clients are? If you are a dedicated designer, you are happy to show off your design prowess and to share experiences with your clients. Find a way to use your downtime, either in contributing to a project in the community or being around your potential clients. Designers who are able to do this often are able to build close relationships with clients, relationships that support them in longterm client development. This is what we all want, and the question is how can we develop this relationship?

One way is to share part of our clients' lifestyles, some of their charities, social events, or simple everyday activities. So look at where you are spending your time. Is there a place or a way that allows you to accomplish some of the things that you enjoy or need to do, while establishing communication with potential clients?

Public relations includes participating in community activities, going to Chamber of Commerce meetings, the historical society, and other community projects, especially those that relate to our potential business. Even where you do your grocery shopping or where you exercise can turn into a public relations effort. A group of male designers gets most of their business by going to the YMCA at noon time. They meet other business people on an informal basis, some of whom develop into clients.

Find some common interest with your potential clients: play tennis, do aerobics, jog . . . Clearly, if you aren't interested in an activity or if it isn't appropriate, don't do it. For example, it will be hard to appear actively interested in the PTA if you don't have children! Find an activity that complements you.

Remember, to develop a client takes a minimum of seven to nine meetings. If you can do it informally at the country club or during another activity, you are likely to build rapport and a structure on which you can base that large sale.

Make it a point to meet people. Leave your studio for lunch. Go to dinner with people. Be seen. Donate your services to a charity function so that you can share a client's special interest.

CREATING PUBLICITY WITH SPECIAL EVENTS

One of the most successful methods of publicizing your work to the right potential client is to have a party at the just-completed project of an existing client. Our clients love to celebrate with us. It gives them the opportunity to show off the space they're so proud of, and it also introduces the designer to many new potential clients.

While working on the project, suggest to the clients that they give a party when the job is complete. This gives the client something to look forward to while things are confused and out of synch, and it encourages craftspeople to finish the project by a specific date.

Ask your clients to think about their prospective guest lists, and offer to help with the party's arrangements by furnishing the champagne, or the food or the flowers, or any number of these things. Share the overall expense with them. You might also suggest that you will show them how to present this space—how to "dress it in party clothes." If they agree, you can set it up, creating the format for their future parties.

This method is very successful for our firm. Very often we will train the staff to explain special details of the job as they take guests on a tour of the finished project. It's an effective way to use that just-completed design as a promotional vehicle.

HOLD A STUDENT CAREER DAY

Holding a career day for high school students and their parents can be good public relations for a design firm. Prepare for it by creating a display of your work and making some notes for a talk on the interior design field. Students benefit from contact with a professional in a service industry: you become in effect a career counselor.

You benefit in many ways. The career day presentation creates good will; it is seen as a contribution to the community. It brings in the parents, giving them first-hand knowledge of the quality of your work. It can also aid in future recruiting of student assistants to work in your studio.

USE YOUR STUDIO

When your studio meets your standards and fits your image as a design professional, use it. Use it as a place to make some of those seven to nine contacts required to make a sale. Your studio is an excellent place in which to demonstrate your work efficiency. Find ways to bring people in to see your studio—not just your clients, but people you would like to meet.

You may also offer your studio as a meeting place for a community group of which you're a member. Place examples of your work strategically so that they are noticed by people who walk into your conference room. This allows you to introduce your services casually to people who may have no idea what designers are about.

Sometimes it is easier to get and keep the full attention of your client when you schedule a meeting for a mealtime. If possible, set it up in your studio presentation area or conference room, and have it catered. This allows you to devote the entire meeting to the subject of design.

Establish a time schedule and stick to it. Let the client know that lunch will be served at noon and that he will be finished by 1:30. Because so many people have special diets, check your client's preferences in advance.

Keep the materials needed for the presentation separate from the food. Either make your presentation first and serve the meal later, or serve first and present later. Even the most beautiful samples lose their effectiveness when smeared with food.

There should be at least one small design touch that sets this meal apart from the average business meal—the tablesetting, placement of food, napkins—any small but interesting touch.

SEMINARS OR CLINICS

Very often, design studios will present seminars to their clients and the community on subjects ranging from historic preservation and Victorian decor to environmental issues and more. If your firm sponsors a program on an appropriate subject, it boosts your credibility. It shows your audience that you understand what makes up a quality presentation on that specific subject. Don't hesitate to use outside consultants; a good presentation only adds to your firm's prestige.

A successful seminar, one that builds goodwill, has several key elements. The first element is planning. Decide on the size of your target audience, whether you will present a single program or a series, and whether you will charge. It is usually wise to charge for these programs in some way. If people pay a fee, they are inclined to be sure that they don't miss any of the programs. People tend not to value what is given freely.

The topic must be appropriate to your firm. If your clientele loves Early American, Colonial, and inherited antiques, a seminar on the correct use of battered cement pedestals and chicken wire as decorative elements probably won't go over too well. Likewise, if the seminar is dedicated to do-it-yourselfers, it's not appropriate if you are trying to develop clients for your firm. If the audience is comprised of facilities managers, the topic can be technical. It is best to look at your potential clients and to gear the subjects to their particular interests.

Choose the right setting. If you plan the talk as an informal gathering, your studio conference room may be large enough. If you open the talk to the public, it may be necessary to rent a space. Hold the seminar in an appropriate facility, so that the people attending are comfortable. We are designers; therefore, people attending a program of ours expect to come to a reasonably good space. They expect comfortable chairs. They expect controlled temperatures and audio-visual equipment. They know that as designers we know the difference between so-so and just-right; anything less will only cause problems.

If you work out a suggested program or group of seminars, you may want to use this as a fundraiser for a charity. It not only gives you a new potential list of clients, but it also shows that you are very committed to a local charity or program. This, therefore, helps build that network of people which encourages the development of our practices.

Present the programs professionally. You may want to bring in an expert. Then, if something is said that causes your clients to take offense, you won't be blamed. After all, you didn't say it; you just provided the forum.

For a series, you need a group of good professional speakers. Few speakers can handle a long seminar themselves unless they have been highly trained. Breaking the seminar into teams can ease the pressure. Find a star. Find people who are experts in their fields, and let them talk about their specialties. If you are a well-trained public speaker, maybe you should handle the presentation. If not, find somebody else who is qualified and appropriately trained for this.

People who attend your seminar will have the opportunity to meet many of your staff people and the people of your group. If you bring in an expert speaker, that leaves you and your staff free to talk to the individuals who attend. It gives you a chance to meet these people and to interact on a subject in which both of you are very interested.

If you are the expert speaker, consider what your message is when designing your speech. What point do you want to make? What thought do you want your audience to take away with them? Use this as your beginning because you want to leave that audience with a clear idea of the purpose of the speech. Then build on it.

(For more on public speaking, see Part 2.)

NETWORKING

It is not so much what you know, but who you know, and how you use those contacts that counts. The process of developing and using your contacts for informal advice and moral support as you pursue your career is called networking. Through it, you can learn about jobs, people and situations that credit reports do not cover. With a good networking system, it is easier to find the right type of client.

Each of us has been involved in at least one networking project. Some have been productive and worthwhile and others really just don't make it. Effective networking must have a goal, a strategy, and a direction. The basis for a networking system is your list of friends, a telephone book, your correspondence files, and your address book.

First of all, for a networking system to work, you must make regular contact. You may meet every Tuesday morning for breakfast, and at that breakfast, each of you should bring at least one lead. This is a requirement: you don't go to the meeting unless you can suggest a lead for one of the other people at the table. Exchanging updates on every member's activities paves the way for more useful conversation.

Don't be afraid to make the first contact. If specific people would be good contacts, be assertive. Make a phone call; say hello; talk to them at a meeting. Explain your position and the ways you could work together. Make a referral and bring them a client. Then they owe you one.

Ask the right questions. You are there to find out what is happening in the field: what's new, what's terrific, and who's doing something—who could use you. You can probably acquire some information about anything just by contacting four or five people and asking where you can find a particular craft or item. People like to be considered authorities. So ask the right questions. This is not just a social visit; it is an opportunity to develop business.

It's also valuable to network with your competitors. Understanding their trends helps us know how to compete with them. If they've added twenty-four people to pursue business with doctors, maybe we should consider another arena. There are many ways to share information without jeopardizing your business. Good relationships with your fellow designers can save you a lot of aggravation and money by simply sharing tips.

Stay in touch. Meet regularly. Sometimes it's better not to start a relationship if you can't keep it up on a four-to-six-week basis. Send articles out of the newspaper to members of your group. Do anything you can to let the people in your group know you're still interested in them.

Send birthday and anniversary cards. If you can learn these dates for your contacts, keep them in a book and organize your mailings by month.

Send thank-you notes when someone does you a favor. A handwritten note makes more of an impact than a verbal thank you, but that is important too.

Promote other people. You accumulate good will by introducing people to each other and recommending them for projects. When I meet people who are good in their disciplines, I try to introduce them to the right people in the right situations.

Work at enlarging that network. Usually introducing people to a network makes it stronger; however, if it gets too large, it's not as effective.

Finally, evaluate the results. Have you received any business from being in this network? What type of referrals are you getting, and how much time are you spending on this program? Is it worth your investment in time? If you find that you've made eight or ten visits and come up empty-handed, perhaps you are in the wrong networking group.

Evaluate the people. The most valuable people understand your practice and may have worked with you. A good network contains people who are exposed to potential projects at the right time in order to be valuable to you. Which time is right depends on your specialty. If the project has progressed too far for your services to be needed or there is already a designer involved, there is no point in asking for leads. If you have made changes in your firm in the last year, or key people in the network have changed their positions and no longer have access to information you can use, you may need a different network.

Who are the people who have access to information at the right time? Real estate agents know of clients looking for property; developers know of companies considering a move to a new building. Financial specialists look for money resources for new projects. Headhunters—employment agencies—know of companies planning to grow. We need clients who are making changes and our network team needs to be involved in and understand these changes.

Start a "good lead" club made up of people who are targeting the same type of client. This might include interior designers, architects, engineers, landscape architects, contractors, and suppliers. The type of design work you all do should be for similar clients. You may even work as a team on some projects.

Formal networking is not for everyone. You can derive some of the same benefits by asking the consultants you work with to introduce you to their clients, and offering to do the same for them. Having lunch with, or keeping in close contact with, an industry person who "knows it all" can keep you abreast of new projects and directions that could help you in your marketing.

SHOW HOUSES

Show houses give you an opportunity to present your talents and expose your work to people who want to see quality furnishing or are interested in retaining a designer. Participating in a show house can be a strong marketing move if it is appropriate for your practice and if show houses are presented well in your area.

Before you commit your firm to participating in a show house, find out what rules and regulations apply. Also check on the coordinators. Have they run a show house before? What are their responsibilities? Some show houses ask you to staff the rooms; others insist your work speak for itself.

Participating in a show house is expensive, which can be a major drawback to using this method of marketing. If you elect to participate in a show house, take the time to do it well so that it is representative of your work. One of the advantages is that you control the project and can design anything you like: a barrier-free room for use by the physically challenged, an office, playroom, or home exercise center. You have a responsibility to educate the public, to show that designers can understand their particular needs. At the same time, you need quality control and your room must entertain because people go to a show house for the fun of it. The resulting room may be something you want to photograph for your portfolio.

The personal interaction is valuable. There may be as many as a thousand or more volunteers working with designers in the house—a thousand people who are potential clients or who may lead you to potential clients. Often, a design group shares sponsorship with a charity. This adds an emotional appeal to the project, making it seem community-oriented rather than just a commercial venture to showcase design talent.

Designers who participate in show houses are usually selected by a board of directors, people who often hold social positions within the community. It takes a great deal of effort and time to do a showhouse. Usually the commitment is just about a year, from planning to completion. Check your schedule and be sure you have the stamina.

Room allocation is often determined by a selection board or by chance. If you have a choice, consider both its accessibility to visitors and its photographic qualities. Take note of the condition of the room. You may be responsible for restoring it to its original condition at the close of the showhouse. Or it may need repairs before it can be used. Take this into consideration before you commit to doing a showhouse room. Be sure you know exactly what you are getting into before you start.

There should be a contract between you or your association and the charity. The coordination structure should be in place. The committee of a show house customarily has a general chairman who will organize the entire project and the volunteer structure. This person heads and controls all other committees. Real estate matters—procuring the house and determining what agreements are required between the owner, design team, and charity—are handled by another person. A third person handles financial aspects, ensuring that all monies coming into the project are dedicated appropriately for pre-specified expenses or that they go directly to the charity. Any mismanagement of funding can cast a bad light on all the participants.

You should check legal issues. Will you be held liable for events beyond your control? A lawyer should be involved to ensure that appropriate permits and liability issues are covered. You also need a lease. The attorney and accountant will take care of taxes and other state requirements.

Normally, the show house will provide you with liability insurance, but it is up to you to talk to your insurance agent to see that the materials used in your room are properly insured for the time they are there. It is least expensive to add this onto your existing policy.

When you participate in a charity show house, it is usually at no expense to the organization: you are responsible for all expenses for your room.

In metropolitan areas, many wholesale sources will supply designers with products to use in show house displays, which reduces the cost. The show house staff will have a list of sources willing to supply paint, carpeting, furnishings, electrical fixtures, and even services such as paperhanging and carpentry. This list should be made available to you when you are negotiating to design a room within a show house. Away from cities with design centers, these arrangements are generally not available.

A good house for a show house will provide easy traffic flow in order to accommodate the circulation of a thousand or more people per day. Parking is critical. If people can't park their cars and access isn't easy, this discourages people from coming.

Is the house properly prepared and heated, if necessary? Are there public toilets and is the electricity and plumbing appropriate? Usually, the house will be open during some evening hours, so lighting is important. Designers are responsible for cleaning and maintaining their own rooms, but make sure you know in advance what is expected of you.

Twenty-four hour security should be provided. One or more security people should be available at all hours before the show house is open. Often, these are off-duty policemen.

Publicity is one of the main reasons designers participate in show houses. Before committing yourself and your staff to the project, ask what publicity structure is in place. Sometimes a celebrity is brought in for publicity value. Perhaps a local advertising agency has donated its services, or an experienced publicity committee is involved. The chairman should be a good writer and communicator. Ask when press releases will be mailed and who is to receive them. You may be able to add key names or publications to the list. Close ties to local magazines and newspapers enhances the value of the project.

How will photography be handled? Some show houses designate a preferred photographer who offers a special rate. Sometimes magazines and newspapers send their own photographers. Can you arrange to share the cost of photography with one of the major resources for your room? Will you have access to the show house at night in order to photograph?

All press releases should include a telephone number and contact person the media can call for further information. The person or committee who handles publicity often contacts national magazines, inviting them to see the house. The resources who donated the furnishings will often alert individual editors.

To encourage visitors, special rates should be listed for groups in promotional materials; the committee can also encourage group visitations by offering transportation and lunches. Investigate what other activities are offered in the region while the show house will be open. Perhaps the show house organizers can arrange a tie-in promotion with them.

The printed program should be of good quality. Look at past program books for the quality of their graphic design and their intended use. People keep these books and refer to them to remember the rooms and designers, as well as products and sources. The program can acquaint prospective clients with a good resource list useful for many years to come. If you design a room, invest in an ad. If you decide against doing a room, the showhouse program is a good place to address potential clients.

A show house is usually open six or seven days a week. Ideally, you or a member of your firm should be allowed to staff the room; then you can hear what people have to say about it. Some show houses will not permit designers to be present after the show house opens (except to clean the room), and I feel this is a drawback.

There will often be a sales office on site where people can purchase items from the rooms. Any charity involved is customarily given a ten percent or more commission on any of the items sold. Other items may be donated to be sold on a cash basis.

Charity show houses open with a preview party, usually attended by each sponsor and designer. This can be expensive, but the proceeds go directly to the charity and the cost is tax-deductible. Money is also raised through auctions and raffles of furniture and furnishings items. The renowned Kips Bay showhouse in New York City auctions a completely furnished doll house each year.

To get the most out of your show house experience, keep a list of the people you worked with on it and keep in touch. You've developed some strong relationships, and they can become a part of the networking and marketing plan for your firm.

HOW TO GET PUBLISHED

You don't have to be a celebrity to have your name in the newspaper. All it takes is a letter or phone call to the local newspaper when an appropriate situation comes along. Perhaps you've just completed a remodeling project for a retail store client. Articles that mention your firm, that are written about your firm, or that are written by individuals in your firm, can reach more than one potential market. Reprints can be mailed to your list of prospective clients or become part of presentations for appropriate projects.

Try to get your work published where it will be seen first by potential clients. Local newspapers and consumer-oriented magazines are more likely to present you to the right audience than are professional design journals, which are read primarily by your peers. There are magazines for every interest: lighting, bathrooms, kitchens, Victoriana, country decor . . . Don't forget trade journals covering your client's business. Whether the subject is accounting, nursing or zookeeping, you will find a magazine that covers it. Libraries have books listing magazines by type.

Research which magazines are appropriate for your special project and what their publication requirements are. ASID's pamphlet, *How to Get Your Work Published,* includes a list of magazines that publish design work, along with their addresses, and requirements. In all cases, it helps to double-check the editor's name with a phone call. A correctly-addressed, well-photographed project will prejudice an editor in your favor.

Read three to six issues of the magazine in which you would like your work to appear. This gives you a good idea of the range of what is acceptable to the editors. Write and ask for their editorial schedule for the year.

When interior designers talk about being published, what we usually mean is photography and an article on that project. Check with the magazine to see what special requirements they may have regarding artwork. Some want 35mm slides; others insist on 4 × 5-inch transparencies. Keep in mind that vertical shots are almost always used for covers.

Often, editors will suggest two or three photographers if you ask for recommendations. Don't be surprised if an editor tells you the magazine will only consider work by a specific photographer. The magazine may be using a photographer's judgement to screen projects that don't fit its needs.

If you think a project may interest an editor, it is permissible to send Polaroids or snapshots to determine their level of interest before you invest thousands of dollars in professional photography. You need written permission from the client if you intend to publish photography of their project. Most magazines will not consider publishing a project without this written release. You also need a release from the photographer.

Once you have the photography and it is in the proper format, prepare a list of resources and technical details for the project. It doesn't hurt to include your own well-written description of the project: its goals and problems, and what was achieved by your design. Include the name of the photographer in your write-up; it could get you noticed. Editors may know the photographer's work, even though they are unfamiliar with yours.

If you plan to write an article, the topic you choose should be one you have researched and with which you are comfortable. (For more on this, see Public Speaking in Part 2.) Consider the publication. Most of us work within a limited geographic range and would not benefit that much from national circulation. Design trade publications, which may be easy to break into, simply expose details of your working arrangements to your competition. This is not the vehicle in which to meet your clients. It is usually better to be published in a small local newspaper that your clients read, than in a national publication which is beyond their scope of interest.

Very often the articles are used as promotional material by other design studios, and therefore have little marketing potential for the original author of the work. People who pick up such articles use the author as an authority to support their own positions. You can see from the way people use your material that there are many ways in which you can use material written by other people for your own benefit.

Sometimes an article cut from a newspaper can be sent to a client with a comment added. This may reinforce your particular theories more effectively than something you wrote yourself.

PUBLICITY

Make a point of meeting the editors and writers of your local newspapers and area magazines. Volunteer your expertise in design matters; the next time they need a design term clarified, they may call you. This builds a relationship that may escalate to your being quoted as a source within articles, and may eventually lead to an article on your firm or your clients. But don't expect quick results. Magazines work on a one- to nine-month lead time, and people rarely act immediately on what they read. They may carry around a clipping for years before they can afford to hire a designer.

THE PUBLIC RELATIONS PROFESSIONAL

A professional public relations person develops relationships with editors in the same way as a designer might but on a broader scale, and usually for more than one interior designer. Professional publicists network constantly to keep up on what editors want and can use. They function as go-betweens to smooth the flow of information from those who have it, to those who need it or might use it.

What should be publicized? Anything that is news: a new client, a completed project, a new direction for the firm— some kind of growth or change. Sometimes you initiate the flow with a press release on a project with a client. Sometimes the publicist calls you with a specific request from an editor. In either case, you have no control over the end use of your material. Once it leaves your office, it is out of your hands. If you need control, advertise.

Should you hire a publicist? It's a great idea, if you can afford it. Today they cost a minimum of $5000 a month for a good person; plan on sticking with a good publicist for at least a three-year period, or don't begin. It is possible to hire publicists for shorter spans of time, or on a per project basis, but it doesn't always pay to do so: ordinarily they don't know very much about your firm, interior design or how to present a designer. Hiring a publicist is an investment in time as well as money.

Publicists are most useful when you consistently do spectacular work and/or have new products and ideas to communicate throughout the year. When you receive so many requests for information and photography that it interferes with your ability to run your studio, then you need a publicist to sort out which requests deserve your personal attention.

It is much easier for publicists to work with products than with individuals; there is less for the publicist to learn. Public relations for interior designers can be quite expensive, and it takes just the right person. But you don't have to do it alone. One chapter of ASID, the American Society of Interior Designers, hired a publicist to cover the whole chapter. As its members completed projects, they informed the publicist, who in turn tried to place them with editors. This worked very well.

HIGH IMPACT PUBLIC RELATIONS AT LOW COST

Most large or national product manufacturers have public relations programs, for which they need photography of products in use. Manufacturers of carpeting, laminates, wallcovering, and tile usually have such a program. Manufacturer associations, such as the National Association of Mirror Manufacturers, the Marble Institute of America, the International Linen Promotion Commission, and The Wool Bureau all have public relations programs. By working with your resources, it is possible to achieve the kind of exposure that no interior design firm could afford.

When a product manufacturer photographs a design project, it is usually because his or her product is predominant, if not used exclusively. Some designers specify projects with this in mind. If your project meets the manufacturer's standards and fills a need, the manufacturer may offer photographs of it to a magazine, or include your work in publicity packets for newspapers and news syndicates. These publications will often contact you for further information.

If specific product manufacturers do not choose to publicize your work, and if it does not fit into any of the categories of available design competitions, this does not mean your work cannot be publicized. However, you may have to hire a photographer and contact the editors yourself.

Consider entering contests. Often, organizations that promote specific products also sponsor design contests for installations using that product. You don't even need to win to attract the attention of editors because many ask to see every entry, not just the top five. Entering design contests offers a chance to see photographs of your projects in every magazine throughout the nation. Most clients love the exposure and it gives you tremendous exposure, too. There is no way that most of us could pay for this type of exposure, but there is a cost in the time and effort it takes to prepare professional contest entries.

Awards are also valuable. If you have received an award recently from any source, make sure that your clients know about it. It doesn't matter whether the award is from a local

Chamber of Commerce or a major national competition. Your clients are happy to hear of it because it validates their faith in you. Work with the award sponsor by providing them with names and addresses of publications that should hear about the award. This is good for both you and the sponsor.

SPECIALTY SHOPS

Specialty shops make buying easy and fun for clients. They can select a store based on their distinctive needs or style preferences. There is such a wide market that clients become so confused. In specialty shops they find what they want easily. The trend today is toward specialty shops; this is also true in the design field. It is just as hard for you to find the client who likes your particular style as it is for the client to find you. By having a specialized shop you have identified your firm as a specialist.

There is so much to choose from, and clients' tastes are educated by magazines, television, other peoples' homes and offices, show houses, and more. The specialty shop presents a design style in infinite detail, right down to the accessories. Shopping in specialty stores is easy and fun, and that is what buying from designers should be.

Some specialty shops are franchised. If you open a franchised shop today, you have about a 95 percent chance of success. If you start an individual shop and style it yourself, you stand about a five to ten percent chance of succeeding. Franchise lines are styled and made in bulk. There is an opportunity for lower prices and rapid delivery, even for exclusive items not available through regular sources. The lines are usually broad enough to allow for creativity.

DIRECT MAIL

Direct mail is the most selective method of advertising and promotion. It consists of any advertising or promotional materials
that a firm sends to a prospective client. Some firms produce
newsletters; others use a newsy business letter. Even today with
all the junk mail, people still like to receive a well-written business letter. Direct mail, as well as any other type of advertising,
is most effective when done on a continuing basis.

Mailings keep your name in front of both prospective
and past clients. Tell people of your design activities; you
could even send photographs. Send a simple letter or even a
postcard, alerting the client to publicity you might have received. Or sent a reprint of a recent newspaper article on your
work. Plan a year-long program. It need not be expensive, as
long as you are consistent.

Screen those candidates, however, because it is a rare
designer who can afford to do mass mailings. Mailing list
houses say that any response over three percent is excellent.
Use a list of potential clients developed through referrals, past
clients, and personal contacts. Then design a mail program;
you will be sending six to ten pieces to the same person. For
best results, send a series of related pieces, and follow it up
with personal contact by phone or in person.

How well does direct mail work? A firm in California
developed their client list from scratch after moving there
from New York. Within three years they had a very successful
company, just as a result of direct mail. Several firms have
increased their share of the market by sending out promotional
mailings.

Mailing lists targeting a special interest group by profession, neighborhood, and income level are available for a fee

through a number of sources. Dun & Bradstreet now offers such a service. (The section on tools of market research gives more detail on mailing lists.)

ADVERTISING

Advertising and public relations often work together. Some experts view any promotional effort as advertising, whether it is a brochure, your stationery and business cards, or a direct mail campaign to your prospective client list. The graphic presentation for all advertising should reflect the design standards of your firm.

Should you advertise? Advertising is a direct way of presenting your company to your clients. If you use a publicist and you are interviewed by an editor from a magazine or a newspaper, there is always a chance that they will represent you inappropriately. Advertising allows you to present only what you believe people should remember about your firm.

If your firm is new or if you are changing your specialty, advertise. Advertising is a way to keep your name in front of potential clients. Physicians are doing it, attorneys are doing it, and there is a professional way to handle it. Hire a professional to design your ad. Your advertisement should be in keeping with the tone of your firm and your particular segment of the market.

Where should the ads be run? You obtain the greatest advertising impact from publications with the appropriate audience. A publication's audience is made up of those individuals who are interested in, and responsive to, a particular advertising vehicle. Your ads should run in the trade publications of the professionals you want to reach, in local newspapers, and in the programs of show houses if these are popular in your area.

How frequently you advertise is up to you, but professionals suggest that advertising is most effective when it is consistent. If you will be advertising frequently, find an agent who will work with you. "Frequency," the number of times you advertise during a specific period, and "circulation," the number of copies of a publication sold or distributed during a specific period, are terms agencies use. A firm that advertises infrequently and only in low-circulation publications is probably a small account.

Even though you may be a small account, there are also small agencies that will work with you to develop your public relations and advertising objectives. Ad agencies will sometimes make suggestions about ad placement, bringing to your attention publications you might not have known existed.

A good advertising agency for a design firm has handled similar accounts in other fields, or at least a company of the same size. A firm that handles only large accounts will not find your firm very interesting. There is no point in interviewing fifty agencies, but try to see three or four so that you have a basis for comparison. Schedule a session with the agencies. Let them come into your studio, meet your staff, and see what you're all about. Before making your final choice of advertising agencies, talk with other companies that have used a specific agency.

Give your agency an outline of your company history, as well as copies of any other advertisements you may have run and of articles written about your firm. Provide any information that demonstrates how you relate to your clients and to the public. Anything on paper is valuable. It acquaints the agency with the kind of information you want to give out, and with how you look to the media.

Designate one person on your staff to be responsible for working with the advertising agency. The ideal person has an in-depth knowledge of your firm, so he or she can comfortably discuss it. This person will act as the liaison, gathering information and forwarding it to the agency as it is needed.

Once the agency has all this information, ask them how they would handle your account. Ask for a budget recommendation. Most agencies want to work on a yearly basis. A well-coordinated advertising program deserves at least a year-long plan.

Normally, the advertising agent will need to return to his or her office to put together some suggestions. These suggestions should be reviewed by the CEO, your advertising liaison, and one or two other primary people. Visit the agency's office and see how they work. Review the budget and establish priorities.

You may wish to start with a small project and see the results, rather than committing to a long-term relationship. Create a general plan and budget for the year, then make a more precise plan and budget for six months. For my firm, planning a complete format of advertising and public relations programs, and coordinating them with staff activities has worked best. Decide what you want to promote in the next six-month period and how you want your money spent, then put it into a format which you can discuss with your advertising agent or consultant.

Advertising and public relations are investments which do not carry a guaranteed response. In the end, however, investing in a well-planned program proves worthwhile. When a company that had run continual advertisements stopped, eventually the work slowed down. So in order to keep your name in front of your public and to reinforce your image, some form of public relations and advertising is necessary.

Chapter 9

Who Will Lead?

Design firms must have a committed client focus at all times in order to stay profitable. We need to do more than entice or educate, but try, really exert effort to find out what our clients are thinking and then to base our presentations on their wants and desires.

The Japanese have been very successful at this in our country. They deliver and they deliver fast. Nordstrom is known for its high quality customer service. Its goals are in line with its customers': value, a great shopping experience, and great customer service. Every staff member is invested in this mission.

The design company must be seen as a friend or a team member. There must be trust, an understanding relationship that can weather all types of trials . . . an honest relationship built on respect. Each tries to do the best for each other.

Do everything you can to have your clients see your relationship as dedicated to their best interests. Keep excitement level high. Keep your studio attractive, fresh, and new-looking.

Don't use slow times as an excuse to stop advertising or

promoting, even though the budget is tight. Use your creativity to design a way to continue to promote your image. Select a person to take the responsibility to manage your marketing program, and someone to provide leadership. These roles could be performed by two people, but who is best suited to do so? If no one on your staff fits the role, perhaps your next investment should be in someone who does.

The leader must see this as a special opportunity and should believe it is the *most important* mission of his career.

The leader must have a vision of the future of the field and the firm's position in it. The vision must be within the market development area: what will this program do for the firm and how will it complement the working process? That person must understand the business environment and be able to see where your firm fits into this environment.

The leader must be a team builder; a good plan is a product of the team.
The leader must have great communication skills.
The leader must lead by example. It's easy to do something new when you have seen it done before.
The leader must be able to keep everyone motivated.
The leader must be able to keep the program focused.
The leader must measure results.
The leader must find appropriate ways of acknowledging and rewarding achievement.

While the leader supplies the vision and fire, a manager's role is equally important. Plans and fervor aren't enough. The manager makes the program work and adjusts it when necessary. If one person cannot make a phone call, the manager decides who is the next best person to do it. The manager sees to it that day-to-day goals are met and that the program stays on target. If your program entails more paperwork or a different paperflow, the manager makes it happen. When a public relations firm or an advertising agency is involved, the manager is usually the liaison.

The manager keeps the program on schedule and makes sure people and supplies are ready so the firm stays on target.

THE EXTENDED TEAM

One of the key directions of the nineties is the extended team. The team effort doesn't stop at the design services level. It must include the client, consultants, craftspeople, and perhaps the manufacturer. No single discipline can produce the perfect product alone. Interior design is a sophisticated, technological and scientific discipline. Only the well-coordinated efforts of the design production staff and corporate management of the design team can bring the end product to the high level needed to meet the progressive demands of the nineties.

To understand the future directions of the clients, the design team must have information from the client company's strategic management group. The consulting designers need to extend the resources of in-house designers and facility management staff to meet the many changing demands, even after the project is finished.

Computer and modem linkups can speed interaction between client and all design consultants, whether they are large multi-service firms or single person specialists. Some large firms with facility management departments will only work with interior designers and architects who use a specific CAD program. This may affect your decision on what kind of computer to purchase.

You have to allow for ongoing changes when you structure your relationship with the client. Whether the client is buying products or the firm is selling it, purchasing needs to be addressed. For routine replacement of furnishings, it can be less effective for a facility manager to write a furnishing contract with a vendor he has never worked with before, than to do so through the designer who has used that vendor on a regular basis. Obviously this affects what you specify.

Even the product manufacturers are adopting a team approach. Some resources offer to coordinate their products to coordinate with other materials that will be used in that project. Mergers and acquisitions within the office furniture industry mean that we can go to a single firm for seating, workstations, and free-standing desks.

Many people come into the design field because they want to work alone, but this is not the best time for one-man bands. The economic climate suggests that the best and most profitable way to run a firm, and to give the client the best project, is with a good working team.

Working in a team is one of the leadership directions of the design field in the nineties. When you have people working with you, you can't just tell them what to do. It's a question of setting an example. During the project, it isn't what you say, but the way the client sees the project unfolding, the way it's managed, the way they see you coordinating it—and the responsibility and the position you take from an administrative viewpoint. How is the job working? Can you design this project in a way that it really looks well managed and professionally run? This will do more to bring you new clients than any other thing that you do.

SCHEDULING MARKETING EFFORTS

You should do something that relates to business promotion, marketing, and communicating with clients every day. They are not things you can do just occasionally. If you do them that way, your mindset is not ready for the business of marketing. Also, your practice is less likely to be effective and profitable.

You must devote time each day to certain marketing and sales issues. This is very hard for designers. We get totally involved in a project and when we've finished, we say, "I guess I'd better do some marketing."

No marketing and client development plan works that way. You need to make these activities part of your everyday life. Spend part of every day keeping in touch with your clients, reviewing your projects, seeing how you can stay up-to-date, and keeping those projects coordinated. Telephone ten or more past clients every week; call ten prospective clients each week.

As you work on your business development program, and this is a progressive process, you need to hold meetings regularly and renew that commitment. Make sure that everyone has agreed to buy into it. Ask your staff members to sign up for their parts of the program; let them decide what parts they will play during that next block of time and how they're going to be doing it. At the next meeting the success will be reviewed and evaluated.

Chapter 10

Preparing Marketing Materials

To appeal to your chosen market you will need to update graphics for your stationery, collect letters of commendation, write brochures and sales letters, and arrange for photography or a video for your portfolio. You should also prepare resumes of your major staff members, a history of your projects, and a list of the firm's capabilities. Every item that leaves your office should present your firm in a positive light.

GRAPHICS

Look critically at your business cards and stationery. Do the graphics present the right image for your firm? Graphics have style and date, just as design does. A good logo is distinctive, memorable, and has some relationship to your corporate style. Ask someone experienced in corporate images to review your logo to make sure it conveys the right message about your firm. This isn't something that you should do yourself.

Your logo must work in a variety of locations, from business cards and stationery to ads, and even product labels. It should reproduce on a photocopy. Embossing and white-on-white don't copy, and this can be a problem because clients often make additional copies of presentations. If your graphics are in several colors, they should still be readable when converted to black-and-white. The typeface should be legible and an appropriate style and weight.

One of the first things each client sees is your business or calling card. Cards should be a standard size and include all the basics: your name, title and telephone number; the company name and type of business, and your logo if you have one. Your business card represents you when you and your staff cannot be there. The information should be complete, and the graphics appropriate for your style of business. A novelties saleman may need a card that has fold-out gimmicks; most designers do not.

Your stationery should be of a standard quality and color to accept a correction fluid if you need it. Do not use erasable bond; the typing can smudge. For those of you who have computers and printers, smudges and correction fluid are things of the past. Most of the newer printers can use both fan-fold and single sheets of paper, and offer draft and letter-quality printing. Use reasonably well-designed stationery; it is attractive if stationery and business cards coordinate.

LETTERS OF INTEREST

Once you have appropriate stationery, you can send out letters of interest. When you see a project that's happening down the street, you simply drop them a note. An effective letter of interest includes four main points.

1. You noticed their project and would like to acquaint them with your firm.

2. Your company is prepared to handle some of the details of this project.

3. You have materials and answers to some of their problems.

4. Ask to meet with them to compare your company's abilities with their needs.

Letters of interest can be forerunners for sales letters, which are covered in the section on pre-selling in part 2.

ASK FOR REFERRALS

When you finish an outstanding project and your clients are very proud of the job, it's good marketing to ask your client if they know other people who might benefit from your types of services. Since they have worked with you throughout the project, they understand exactly how your firm works and what you have to offer. Do they know other people who might be able to use your services? In most instances, clients are very happy to recommend you.

ASK FOR A LETTER OF COMMENDATION

A client who is pleased with your work may be willing to write a letter of commendation. Ask clients to explain in this letter how your services have been valuable to them. Some designers ask for several sheets of the client's letterhead stationery, write the letter, and then ask the client to sign it. It's much better, however, if the client agrees to write it in their own style and, of course, on their own letterhead.

Then take your group of letters from bank presidents, corporation heads, residential clients, or whomever, to show to potential clients. Or you may wish to have them photocopied to use in mailings to prospective clients. Many times these letters explain how you fit within their system, and this is very valuable to the potential client.

A letter of commendation for an architectural firm stated: "We chose your design firm because we had seen some of your other projects. We feel we made an excellent choice. Your solutions were extraordinary, imaginative, beautiful, and practical. Our new atmosphere makes working here a pleasure and we are more productive." It was on corporate stationery, signed by the chief executive officer.

Another letter of commendation said simply: "We enjoyed working with your firm. You kept on schedule and displayed pride and professionalism in your efforts to bring us a well-designed project. We are so impressed with your firm that we will recommend you whenever we can."

Using letters of commendation instead of having the new client calling the previous client directly can help you position yourself with a new client. Some designers have a portfolio of these letters to show to new clients. Some even feel it is more valuable than a portfolio of photographs.

PORTFOLIOS

Whether you are a beginning designer or an established professional, your portfolio is an important part of your professional presentation and must be updated constantly. This does not mean that older designs cannot be included. It means that your portfolio must vary according to the client and that it must be representative of your work.

A portfolio may include slides, photographs and brochures. Your design specialty will influence the style and presentation.

Some designers use portfolios a great deal; others don't even have them. Recently, I've found that more clients are asking to see a portfolio, and they are not just corporate clients. An effective portfolio must be representative of your work, which means it can't be something you compiled way back in school; it has to be current. It has to be tailored to the type of work for which you are marketing, so a flexible format is a must. Clients don't want to see projects that don't relate to their business. Vary it according to the client's needs. If you are going to see a banker, don't take country club projects because this isn't what he or she is interested in. Take only examples of financially related institutions that you have designed.

Keep it current. You may want to take a project or two a year and design them specifically for your portfolio. Several design firms will undertake one or two projects a year and charge only for the cost of merchandise, with the understanding that the client will permit the designers total control. It gives the client a great project and the design firm has a project that presents its skills the way they feel they ought to be presented.

BROCHURES

What about brochures? Graphic folders or brochures describing your firm are good advertisements. Are they worthwhile? I think so, but I'm not sure you should spend your whole budget on a brochure. Some brochures can cost ten to sixty thousand dollars or more, and this is not appropriate for small design firms.

Cost is not the main consideration; design is. You might want to work with a graphic designer on this project to develop the look.

The write-up should state your general objectives, your values and a little information about your firm. It might also have a blank page on which notes can be written while discussing a particular issue with a potential client. But design the brochure so that you can replace it every six months because this type of marketing piece does date very quickly. So take into account that you will have to replace it often.

PHOTOGRAPHY

Why should you photograph your work? For a number of reasons: insurance records, an aid to memory, a tool for your marketing program, or possible use in a public relations or advertising campaign. The question should be how, not why. If all you need is a visual record to accompany an inventory for insurance purposes, even a 110mm throw-away camera will take good enough shots. Record shots are often made with an inexpensive 35mm automatic, using slow film, a wide-angle lens, and a tripod. Slow film will give definition and clarity to the photo; the tripod is a must with slow film.

But if you plan to use photographs for publicity or advertising, hire the best photographer you can afford. The better the quality of the photography, the better your work appears to be. Take the time to look at photography in national and regional design magazines, and try to see the differences between professional photography and snapshots.

Good photography has an arresting quality. It takes hold of you and elicits a reaction on an elemental level. Excellent photography can manipulate the way you feel about a subject by changing the way you see it. The magic of photography is achieved with angles, lights, and the photographer's skill. Space looks different through a camera lens. Don't be surprised if you have to move furniture or alter your design just for the photograph. An excellent source of information on interior design photography is Norman McGrath's book, *Photo-*

graphing Buildings Inside and Out, published in 1987 by the Whitney Library of Design. This book has an outstanding outline of details that designers need to consider before photographing a project.

The photography in national design magazines and advertisements represents an investment of several thousand dollars. Not all of your work merits, or even requires, such an elaborate and precise visual record. You might try to get your client to agree to pay half the cost of photography. Clients may be interested in owning these photos for many reasons: for personal records or insurance, or for their own marketing programs.

Most design studios hire professional photographers only for projects they feel have some value for publication, or which make a particular contribution to their portfolios. However, keeping a photographic history of a project from start to finish, either in slides or by simple photographs you take yourself, is worthwhile. These can be incorporated into a video or other types of presentations at a later date.

Consider the final use of your photographs in determining whether you need transparencies, black-and-white shots, or color prints. If you plan to submit photography to a magazine for editorial use or advertising, check the publishing requirements. Don't invest in a form of photography that the publication for which you are aiming cannot use. Today most magazines are pleased to accept 35mm transparencies, although in the recent past they demanded 4 x 5-inch transparencies. These days, even a good quality color print can be acceptable because the technology exists to correct less-than-perfect images.

Interior photography is a specialty and an art form; a skilled amateur may be able to produce arresting photographs that show what you want, but don't count on it. I recommend that you use professional interiors photographers. Cities with design centers usually also have interiors photographers; the cost varies according to locale.

There is no guarantee that you will end up with the perfect photo even when you hire a skilled professional. The quality of a photo depends on the photographer's eye for composition and his or her knowledge of films, cameras, and lighting. An error in choosing film lighting or filters for a job can result in colors that are not true. Almost as important is the skill of the film lab. Sloppy processing can also give your colors unwanted casts.

The interiors photographer must compensate for unique problems. What you see when you look into a room is not what the camera sees. A camera's distortion of small spaces is so extreme that what is seen through the viewfinder as perfectly centered is, in fact, off to one side. This distortion can vary in degree from camera to camera (it is worst with the throw-away cameras), and the distance between the subject and the camera. The skilled photographer knows how to compensate.

You don't need to be a photographer yourself to get good results from a photographer, but you must provide some basic information. No matter how brilliant the photographer is, he or she is not a mindreader. If you don't tell him or her what you expect, don't be surprised when you don't get it. On rare occasions, a photographer is so experienced that he or she will be able to tell you what is important about your space, but don't take this knowledge for granted.

When you are considering photographing a space, review the following points with the photographer:

What spaces are important?
Does the room have a focal point?

What qualities do you wish to capture?

Does it have a particular mood or style that you want that photograph to present?

Do you need a complete room in order to convey this message? If you don't, shots of certain areas will do.

If you are hoping to be in a specific magazine which has special requirements, the photographer needs to know.

If you designed a table to enhance a sculpture, tell the photographer. If you want to emphasize efficient use of space, tell the photographer. Otherwise, you may get photographs that do not help communicate the qualities of your work.

Schedule the photography right away. Interiors change with use; they weather and acquire marks of wear. For example, a carefully placed display of collectibles may be shoved aside to make room for a stack of work brought home from the office.

Interiors are at their best during the first month of the installation. Not all marks of wear can be camouflaged successfully. Be sure that your work is photographed correctly the first time; you probably will not get a second chance. If the work is being photographed for possible publication, bear in mind that it may take several days for the photographer to fine-tune the lighting and the angles.

VIDEOS

Videotaping is an effective way to document projects from beginning to end. With the help of a reasonably good photographer you can create a dramatic and enjoyable presentation, especially if you add color and music. Most clients now prefer video presentations to slide shows. Almost every household in the U.S. has access to a VCR, so this marketing effort can save you time in your initial sales contacts.

Videotape presentations don't have to be costly, although some design firms have invested heavily in this area. Fortunately, videotapes are much less expensive to produce today than they were at one time. Video presentations are useful for about two years. Because they date so quickly, don't put so much money into one that you can't afford to change it with minimal effort. And most videotapes can be altered and updated.

A collection of slides can be worked into a presentation. Clients like to see before-and-after shots. You can take photographs of new products in furniture showrooms or at market and have them built into a simple, short video tape. Leave the tape with potential clients for a day and then pick it up in person. This will familiarize them with your work on their own schedules, and give you the opportunity to discuss it with them while it is still fresh in their minds.

Designs for Comfort

Michael and Isadora Newmann
2633 Ash Lane
Boston, MA 12345

Dear Mr and Mrs. Neumann,

Welcome to the community. We hear that you are building a
new home in the Robbins development on Winding Tree Lane,
and would like to introduce you to our interior design firm,
Designs for Comfort.

Designs for Comfort has worked with several families who
built homes along Winding Tree Lane: Dan and Annette Miller
mentioned that you may be interested in our services.

We can help you design your home to support the way you
live, whether you envision your future home as a haven from
the outside world, as a gathering place for friends and
family, or a cross between the two. We will help you define
your needs and show you how to satisfy them within the
parameters of budget, time and available sources.

Designs for Comfort has helped many families create
environments that meet their unique and individual needs. We
can help you create a home that is yours, not a duplicate of
every other on the block.

I will be calling you within the week, to see if we can set
a time to discuss how Designs for Comfort might meet your
needs.

Sincerely,

Ian Stone
President
Designs for Comfort

Figure 10-1

Designs for Business, Inc.

Dear Mr. Sechelski,

Designs for Business would like to be your design firm when you renovate your health care facility.

Since 1958, our firm has helped concerns such as your own to adapt and update their facilities to make better use of the available space, increasing comfort and efficiency for staff and patients. We have been responsible for space planning and specifying furnishings for more than 200 medical facilities, including patient rooms and adjacent lobbies in two area hospitals, dental and optometric offices, and dormitories for 2,000 students at a residential college.

The staff at Designs for Business includes specialists in planning and design, and we have long-standing working relationships with several local structural and electrical engineering firms, as well as with the architectural firm of Tower & Stone. On the hospital projects, Designs for Business worked with Stevenson Bros., a highly skilled general contracting firm with an excellent record in this state.

To tell you more about our firm, we enclose a brochure, a list of past projects, and a magazine article about our work on a project similar to your own.

Could we schedule a meeting to discuss how Designs for Business can help you? I will be calling you within the week to discuss an appropriate time.

Sincerely,

Ian Stone
President
Designs for Business, Inc.

Figure 10-2

LETTER OF COMMENDATION

Professional Administrative Services

1 2 3 C o m m e r c e S t r e e t • H a r r i s b u r g , P A 1 7 1 1 0

Professional Administrative Services
123 Commerce St.
Harrisburg, PA 17110

To whom it may concern,

We chose the interior design firm of Designs for Business to update and upgrade our clerical spaces and reception room.

Their reputation for producing good work space at a good price is well deserved. Their designers gave us more than attractive offices at a good price: they gave us offices that work better.

We are very proud of our new offices, and definitiely recommend Designs for Business.

Very truly yours,

Isaac Dennison
President

Figure 10-3

Abacus Accounting Network

50 Commerce Street
Harrisburg, PA
17110

Abacus Accounting Network
50 Commerce St.
Harrisburg, PA 17110

To whom it may concern,
Our firm had outgrown its office space, but we felt our
present location was a factor in our success. We called
Designs for Business for a consultation to help us determine
our best options.
The firm sent a space analyst to observe the way we worked,
and asked important questions such as how much of the office
we wanted visitors to see. Designs for Business helped us
define what we really needed: space that worked better, not
more space.

They came up with a plan that allowed us to stay where we
are, and when we decided to proceed, they handled the
project for us with minimal disruption to our workdays.

Our offices run more smoothly and make a great impression
on our clients. Hiring Designs for Business is an investment
we heartily recommend.

Sincerely yours,
Roger Addison
President

Figure 10-4

Chapter 11

What it Takes to Dominate the Field of Design

Becoming a force in the interior design field takes a very clear definition of your strategic objectives. You must go through your mission statement, the objectives and goals of your firm, and decide where you want to be and how you are going to get there. You must understand your firm's abilities and the competitive market so that you can define your objectives clearly.

You need to analyze your segment of the market. How do they make decisions? You must know how they think and just when and how they are going to use your design speciality.

Analyze the competition. Know their strengths and weaknesses and how these compare with your firm.

Identify any elements that will influence your success. What does it take to make you successful? Come up with that list and draw up a plan to make it happen. Decide what is most important and set your priorities. Identify the cost in time, money and effort that it will take to accomplish each element in your success plan. Make sure you know what it will take to do something, and what you should expect in return.

Act on it. There is no point in having a plan unless you are committed to making it happen! Don't let your plan for success be an abstract concept. Decide what action needs to be taken, and how to keep it in constant motion.

PRPPQ-Relative Perceived Product Value. This is a marketing term meaning public opinion. Check on the PRPPQ of design services.

COMMITMENT

When you work for a design firm, you know the excitement of commitment. We are very deeply committed to our design work; we must be as deeply committed to marketing and selling, and to client interaction. Otherwise, we won't be able to put in the energy needed to succeed.

In-depth commitment must radiate throughout the firm. As you work on your business development program, and this is a progressive process, you need to hold regular meetings to renew that resolution. Make sure that everyone has agreed to buy into the program. Don't assign roles; let your staff decide for themselves what they will be doing in the next block of the process.

There is no space in the program for negative people. The leader and all players must be invested or deeply *committed* to the program. They must enjoy the excitement of being part of the team. Leadership is key—this may be the role of the president. If this person is not the right type, find someone who is.

You won't enjoy the process if you don't have that in-depth commitment, and dissatisfaction can radiate throughout the firm. We must all have this commitment as one of our key objectives.

PART 2

SELLING AS COMMUNICATION

Chapter 12

An Introduction to Selling

I wish I could eliminate the word selling from this book; for many of us, sell and selling have so many negative connotations. Selling is an opportunity to build a relationship. I'm not a salesperson; I'm the person who creates the buying opportunity.

Design is an investment, not a casual purchase. Both client and designers must invest in the project; therefore, it is important for both parties to spend sufficient time and research to be sure that it is the right investment for both. The right selection can affect and enhance many areas of our lifestyles.

Selling interior design services requires finding a prospect with a need, want, or desire, demonstrating to that prospect that you have the ability and experience to solve the problem, and converting that prospect into a client. Your portfolio and photographs can be designed to support your communication effort; however, what sells a job is your skill at communicating your firm's ability to do the job. People buy from people, not from pictures.

Selling is an ability that can be acquired and mastered.

It depends on your ability to both understand the particular client, and to build a relationship appropriate to support the structure needed to do the job. Most successful professionals can sell. We are all salespeople from the day we were born, but the question is: do we sell the right things, at the right time, to the right people, to accomplish our goals?

Designers receive little training in communication, yet in almost every instance we must communicate well. There is no design if there is no one to pay for it. Sales are where the money comes from. To work on the kind of projects you want, someone must first promote design services. We must sell throughout the project and make people want to buy from us. And who is better able to present this than the professionals who understand what they are designing?

Some interior designers are excellent communicators. A salesperson has to be positive, enthusiastic, and proud to work for his or her firm. He or she knows and respects the competition, but believes his or her firm will do a better job for the client. Most good salespeople have a lot of drive. They must be willing to do whatever it takes to get a job. They have to keep their enthusiasm high; they cannot allow themselves to be discouraged. Even after they've lost a project or a sale, they are challenged to go on to the next.

Most effective salespeople operate under the K.I.S.S. principle, which means Keep It Short and Simple. Good presentations are prepared with precision, but they are delivered in a short, simple, and direct fashion.

There should be no surprises when you are trying to sell to a client. Make it easy and comfortable. Encourage them to ask questions. The more the client talks, the less you talk and the more you learn about their wants and needs, and the way they think. In a sales conversation, the client should talk 70 to 80 percent of the time and the salesperson 20 to 30 percent. This is the perfect balance.

Learn to listen. Very often, clients know what they want or at least have strong feelings they would like to express. Try to encourage your clients to give information, and to tell you what they think is important. During a sales development conversation, your ability and willingness to listen is crucial. So are your skills of observation. You often pick up visual cues from surroundings or body language.

A good salesperson has developed judgement. When an executive is involved in nine or ten matters simultaneously in his office, it isn't a good time to press for a major decision.

Learn to direct a conversation. In trying to develop rapport, show interest in the clients, but try to keep it related to the issue at hand. Good interviewing techniques build close relationships. Our interactions with clients show whether we have been working on a wavelength that they understand.

To succeed at selling, you must do it every day. You need to set up a schedule of interactions, whether by phone, in person, or through the mail. If you only do so once in awhile, you get out of practice and if there is one thing you need here, it's practice. The client should see the designer as a competent professional and someone whom they can trust with their design problems.

Be proactive: be the first person to call. Schedule your week and your day to allow for a standard time for getting in touch with clients. Of course our business is to respond to needs, but it's more impressive if you can say that you have recognized a potential problem and suggest the issues the client should consider.

• THE PROCESS FOR SELLING •

Market Plan:

> Know your firm
>
> Know your client
>
> Know how to reach client—bridge methods
>
> Build confidence—position the firm

Contacts:

> Meeting them—by phone, person or other direct methods.
>
> Building the confidence, trust, relationship (two-way contacts are the best way to do so)

Observation and Documentation of Needs:

> Combination of knowing your client and research and development required to present an appropriate solution to needs.

Design Work:

> With information supplied, prepare solution that will fit all of the client's needs—design, budget, time, etc.

Presentation:

> You present your solutions to client's problem; show how your firm can solve their needs.

Approval:

> Client approves the solution which has been presented by signing proposal, confirming changes, or whatever is needed for next step.

Confirmation:

> An ongoing effort to be sure the client's needs are met—that they are satisfied. This is constant reinforcement early in job. Follow-up. Keep in touch after the job is finished. (This is also a good way to promote yourself for recommendation to another client).

Referral

SALES FORCE

Sales is a highly skilled, organized profession dedicated to bringing a needed product to a buyer—an interested person able to afford and buy our product. The sales process can vary substantially, depending on the firm's specialty and extent of services.

Many designers don't like to sell. If you are one of these, team up with a partner who *lives* to sell. To succeed at selling, you must find it rewarding. Otherwise, you won't be willing to go that extra mile necessary to win the job.

There was a day when the marketing or sales department for a design firm was considered lower class, not quite professional. It often occupied the last office down the hall. Today, the persons able to bring projects are the highest earners within most firms; they usually dictate the direction of the jobs. Many firms will not employ anyone who does not bring in work. Even the lowest of support staff are expected to be out there generating business.

In many leading firms, the marketing or salesperson is the CEO or another top executive. Very often sales is the highest-paid position within a design firm. The salesperson can determine the direction and the success of the firm. After all, without work, we don't have the opportunity to design.

If selling goes against the grain for you, you ought to find someone who is really excited about it, who enjoys doing it, and who would like to partner with you and work with you to develop your opportunities. I don't necessarily mean partner in the company structure sense; you could partner within a corporate structure, under a business structure, or simply work with a team member. It is so easy to sell someone else, but often difficult to sell yourself.

Who should handle sales? Consider what is most comfortable for you, but recognize that part of the process of presenting your firm requires you to have a sales force ready, and that all key performers must be ready to play their parts. Once you find the potential clients and know where your firm is going and what services are appropriate for you to render, then decide who will carry out this particular effort. You must have your system ready.

Each person in your firm should play some position on your sales force or marketing team. Each person has abilities and areas in which they would have some outside involvement. Although they may not be marketing director material, they still play part of the team. Marketing requires a total team investment.

TEAM OR PARTNER SELLING

Selling can often be more effective and more fun when you work as part of a team. Yes, it may take a lot of effort to get used to working with your partner, but once you develop a rapport, you'll practically know the exact word they will say next. You'll know what move they will make next and you'll know exactly how to develop your presentation so that it really bonds the client to your firm.

Look at your organization and see if you would perform better as a team member instead of alone. Then decide which members will relate best to the client, and which members know each others' ways well enough to develop mutually complementary styles. This takes experience and practice.

Buckminster Fuller talks about synergistic issues where two or more people working together can do the work of five or six. Sometimes two people produce less than the work of one. In a good situation, team work can lead to more exciting selling and presentation formats. It helps to sell your services because it is generally more interesting to the client and shows the teamwork process.

PROBLEM-SOLVING

Problem-solving is one of the strongest sales tools in today's market. Clients are looking for firms that can take care of their problems, and most clients believe that their problem is totally exclusive to them. The client believes that no one else in the world could ever have imagined their particular problem.

In fact, most of the problems we encounter are typical for certain situations, and we can almost guess in advance what the problems will be. But to this client, it is unique. This is the first time it has happened to them. Allow them this feeling, but also bring them to realize that you understand their problem, and that you are accustomed to dealing with situations of this sort because your job is to solve their problems.

You have to bring clients slowly to the realization that you are equipped and prepared to handle all sorts of problems. This means taking care to explain in detail how just one change in their businesses or lifestyles may mean that what worked fine before may no longer work as well. For example, ten people cannot work in a space meant for six, nor can six work as effectively in a space designed for ten. There are too many wasted movements.

ATTITUDE

Attitude and approach are essential elements of selling. Be able to relate your product to something the client understands. A good example of this is how a particular furniture manufacturer addressed business people through a magazine article. When asked the purpose of office furniture by *Success Magazine* (July/August 1991), Richard "Dick" G. Haworth said, "It's a management tool. It helps people do their jobs. It transmits a culture of a company." His statement makes people think differently about furniture, makes office furniture a management tool instead of a bland necessity. Thus, office furniture becomes more desirable. Remember, selling is educating the customer so that he or she wants what you are selling, then turning that want into a need. Haworth's statement brings life and activity into furniture; it's part of the company's management system.

Spending time with clients is invaluable. Haworth, president of Haworth Inc., also suggests that salespeople see clients in person as often as possible. Although technology in the form of telephones, faxes and modems is wonderful, it does not replace personal interaction. Haworth feels it is important to stay stimulated by the customer.

The way we feel about design and our firm radiates from every motion we make. Clients speak to us with their body movements; we project our feelings and attitudes in the same way. If you are not up and ready, it is best to stay away from that "special" client. We schedule these personal visits to enrich our opportunities. So spend time and effort to be sure you are really in the right, positive frame of mind.

Design is valuable. Keep this firmly in mind.

A very successful designer told me that a prospective client had informed him that she had a resale which enabled her to buy the same things as he could buy in the design centers—so why did she need him?

In his gentlemanly Southern style he replied, "Honey, you don't have any idea of what to buy, and you don't have any idea of what to do with what you buy."

Most often, all a client with a resale number will do is spend money and receive no value.

Good design and great project management add great value to a project. With the right designer, clients don't waste money on wrong selections or mistakes. They *invest* money carefully.

Chapter 13

The Client Comes First

"Customers use our time up until their decision to buy. After that we are using *their* time. Therefore, we must deliver immediately." The objective is to shorten the time between their decision to buy and completion of the job. (Stanley M. David, 1987, *Future Perfect,* p. 79. Reading, Mass.: Addison Wesley Publishing.)

Clients are the most important part of any business. We like to think they depend on us, and they do, but without them we have no business. Clients are the core of any business. They come to us with needs and hopes, and it is our job to help them accomplish these.

When they call, you cannot think of it as an interruption. Clients give us an opportunity to work. This is the reason your business exists.

Nordstrom has built their retail stores on the creed: "Existing customers are our most valuable asset. The staff who serve them are their most valuable players." Anyone who has shopped at Nordstrom knows that the policy is strongly felt. It is the people who represent Nordstrom on the sales floor who exemplify store policies.

Keep in mind that your staff represents the company as the clients see it; the CEO isn't the most visible person. Yes, the customer comes first. This attitude starts at the top. Everyone on the staff must believe that customers are the reason the firm exists. Too often, the CEO has been burned out by too many experiences over the years and is not quite as happy as he or she should be in dealing with clients. When this happens, that person should not be there and should not be the leader. Set a clear policy for your firm. You all relate to clients. Dedicate time and effort to reinforcing it.

Acknowledge all types of staff behavior that demonstrate positive actions. Reinforcement is the best way to make this type of action a habit in your firm.

Look for something you can use as a good example in every meeting you have with staff because positive attitudes require constant positive reinforcement.

Customers see themselves as important. They don't like to be treated as second class citizens. Find out their needs and make sure that they are treated well.

- Customers like to buy from people they like.
- If you or your staff are not nice to them, they will use another firm.
- They want what they want when they want it. Often their wants are based on emotion rather than fact. If they feel they need something, they will establish a reason for wanting it.
- They feel that because it's their money, they want to set the rules. You must find a way to tailor your service to their system.
- They will stay with you if they believe they are important in your eyes. You can't forget them if you want to keep them as ongoing clients.
- If they are unhappy, they will tell everyone, so exert every effort to keep them happy.

Dale Carnegie wrote in *How to Win Friends and Influence People,* "People are what they are because they can't possibly be anything else." We need to remind ourselves constantly that they have the right to do things their own ways, in their environments. We can't change them. Either we must learn to work with them or we should find another client.

KNOW YOUR CLIENTS

1. Spend time with them. Talk to them. Ask questions. Learn their ways, what they feel is important, their problems, and their joys.

2. Be sure your firm's telephone manners are what they should be. Check on this regularly. Are the people who answer the phone properly representing you? Consider everything from quality of voice (some voices do not project well over the phone) to volume (is it at a comfortable level that can be understood?) Does the person representing you know about the company? Are your employees giving out the correct information in an appropriate style?

3. Make client service a team process. Be sure that everyone involved in your company is aware of his or her position on the team.

4. Keep in mind that client relations is a lifetime project. You are never off-duty. What you do on your personal time can either build or erode your client base.

5. Find a way to conduct surveys regularly. Ask clients what they want, like, and don't like about your firm. Measure their preferences, desires, objectives. Keep an ongoing record of results.

BUILDING CLIENT LOYALTY

• Know who the client is. Not just the owner, but the staff, their sources and clients. If the client is a hospital, know the staff, patients, visitors and suppliers. The client is not the building, but the people who use it.

- The client must become a team member. He or she must play a part in the design process.
- Your entire staff—not just you, the principal—must know the client, not just by name but well enough to understand their goals and philosophies.
- Create a standard method of communication and an appointed communication schedule. Relationships need constant reinforcement.
- Save your time and the client's by using communication methods that are comfortable and compatible to the way they work and live. Consider paper flow styles. Do they prefer verbal or written communication? Are they set up to receive faxes? What is the best time of day for them for personal visits, phone calls, faxes?
- Keep your promises. Be realistic in setting response dates—and meet them. Don't promise something you can't deliver.
- Record the personal information they give you—this is easy to do on a computer. Use this to build rapport. Send gifts or congratulations, birthday cards, etc. We all like to be acknowledged and celebrated.
- Treat clients as if they were life-long friends. Make every task and interaction suggest that you will be working with them forever.

FIND OUT WHAT IS IMPORTANT TO THE CLIENT

When approaching a client, find out what's important to them. A few weeks ago a contractor told me, "I make sure that I treat all my clients the way I would like to be treated" and I said, "Wrong. Treat your clients the way *they* want to be treated."

He looked at me with a very strange expression, so I explained, "You're really into cars. You've always had very unusual European automobiles and you understand cars. I don't understand cars at all. When I take my car to the garage, I want the mechanic to drive it, check what it needs to fix it, and deliver it to my driveway. That's all I want from him. I don't want all the technical information because I don't understand it. I do want to know that he drove the car and he's sure that it will work for me. I need that reassurance. You don't. You know cars. You will want to know exactly what he found and a detailed description of all the problems."

Consider what is important to the client, not what is important to you. Spend time in the very beginning interviewing that client. Be sure you understand just what their needs are. Then, after outlining their needs, go back to your team and see what you can do to meet those needs.

BE PROACTIVE

Don't just react to clients. Be proactive. You be the one to make the call. They are impatient. Recognize their needs by taking the time to call them with a well-organized agenda. Schedule a convenient time each day for getting in touch with them, and advise the clients so that they know they can expect to hear from you. Doing this allows you to be well-prepared with information and updates. You maintain your image of a professional; you are in control, and the clients feel that you're really on top of the job.

Yes, we do need to respond to clients' demands, but this proactive approach is much easier to control than fielding phone calls at the client's whim. If they do make a request, explain that you and your staff are working on their project now, and that you need to discuss their request with the appropriate people and then get back to them. You recognize the problem the client presents, but you also have time to present other issues that require consideration. Finally, ask, "Does this meet your needs?"

It is not good for any relationship for one side to always be on the defensive. Try to put your firm in a position where it can control the process.

Chapter 14

Rapport

Building a rapport with a client is an essential part of developing a good relationship in any project. Take every opportunity you can to meet with the client face-to-face. Yes, we need to use telephones and other modern technology to communicate with clients; however, nothing can ever replace personal interaction.

Interview the clients in order to bring out their opinions and attitudes toward the project. Learn to listen carefully. You must understand just where they are coming from. Learning to develop their interest through conversation is integral to your success in this project. If the client's main interest in a space is to hold large parties, ask how many parties he or she will have in a year. Then ask what else the space will be used for. Lead the conversation, framing your questions to obtain the information you need, but always refer to the client's main interest.

Having an interest in common with a client often solidifies the relationship. Sometimes you have to work to build rapport. At other times, it just happens; it's serendipity. Several years ago, a young designer was hired by an older couple whose previous interior designer was a design superstar whose reputation preceded him wherever he went. The young designer got along famously with the wife, but despite the designer's good background, the husband seemed unwilling to begin the project. Then the young designer happened to comment on the outstanding collection of rifles in the man's study. Surprised that a young girl would recognize them, the man questioned her. Her father had taught her about guns, still targets, and clay pigeons when she was a child, and that sealed the relationship. A few days later, the wife called and told the young designer that her husband felt she was capable of handling the project.

I like to meet with a new client in person, both to see the project and to have some interaction to lay the groundwork for mutual respect. At this time, you might want to bring your portfolio with histories and examples of other projects that are similar to the client's. It is usually best to keep those illustrations as close to their type of project as possible. So in your initial phone call, ask what they have in mind. Then carefully select the materials you will take to show them.

Define your firm. Explain exactly what you do and what the capabilities of your practice are, and enumerate the types of work for which your firm brings in specialists. (In the Design Service Outline, there is a space for other consultants who are involved in the project. Is there a code specialist, an architect and/or engineer?) Make sure the client understands who is involved.

As you discuss the proposed project, think about what the client wants before you make definitive statements. It is not your job to meet with them and, within an hour, define exactly what you would do on the whole project. The client feels that because you are paid a fee, coming up with a project concept will take some effort. So if you have ideas, hold onto them. Listen to the client, develop the project and take a week or a little longer (depending upon the project), to come up with your solutions. If you come up with the answers too fast, it takes away from your professional credibility.

Speak in terms your clients will understand. It is important to be direct and honest. This is not the time to bring out your best list of professional terms and design jargon—these are professional shorthand and can confuse the client. Don't embarrass your clients. Make them feel comfortable with your firm and your terminology, so that they see you as part of their support team.

As you discuss aspects of the proposed project, keep the client's comments in the forefront. Restate to them what they have given as priorities, and discuss what you will do based on those priorities. You might say, "Based on the selection that you have made, we recommend these items."

Bring the clients' preferences into the project as often as possible. Show them that their priorities are also your priorities, and that you are constantly aware of them. It is a good idea, once they give you priorities, to review those priorities and make sure that they are clearly defined, both in your mind and in the way the client has stated them. Very often, clients lack the ability to communicate well in design terms. If you need to interpret these priorities, take the time to make sure that you and the clients understand what you are supposed to be doing.

Individual clients like to make some decisions. Corporate clients expect you to do a study and to suggest the best options or courses of action. Most clients like to feel that they have made the selections, so present the project with options and choices. Explain your selections and why you feel that certain aspects may be better than others, but still let the client understand why these decisions are made, and give them two or three selections from which to choose. Especially in working with corporate clients, you will find that clients like the responsibility of making their own decisions.

If you give a client a choice of twelve options in an unfamiliar area, they probably will not be able to give you the best decision. When you winnow down these options to the two best and allow clients to choose between them, they feel they are in control. You performed professionally in sorting out the issues and bringing matters down to the point where making a decision was easy. Be very realistic in talking about how much things are going to cost, issues of the construction, and also the time that will be involved. If the project involves a great deal of remodeling, completely changing or altering the use of the facility, and possibly making it unusable for awhile, tell the clients so that they are ready for it.

No client likes to be surprised with a final budget that is two-and-a-half times the original; nor does a client like it when a three-week project turns into a four-month project. Clients need to understand exactly what they are committing to in order for you to keep a good relationship with them. So don't surprise them.

Early in the interview (again, see the Design Service Outline), talk about the client's expectations regarding the time and budget. Sometimes, they feel that this project can be done in just a few weeks and that it's very simple, and yet you know that it will be quite complex. Now, in the early stages of your relationship, is the time to clarify these matters so that the client's expectations are within the realm of your firm's capabilities. From the first time you meet the client, and on throughout the project management phase, schedule weekly phone calls. These scheduled contacts, initiated by you, keep clients up-to-date and will save you a tremendous amount of time in fielding phone calls from the clients. Keep them informed, let them feel that they are part of the job and that are they are very important. Try to make it a point to initiate the call rather than wait for them to call you.

You need to identify the person you will be working for. There should be one person on the job that all information goes through. This will keep the lines of communication clean and clear. The contact person can relay your progress reports to others within their firm and keep everyone informed. This is the best method of retaining rapport with the client.

Who is really responsible for the job? How many people will be involved? What decision-making process is there? Put this type of information on your first page of notes in the client's file, even if you don't use our Design Service Outline. Understanding how the clients make decisions, who they are responsible for or to, and what kind of information they must have to keep their superiors informed, is critical. They may need certain types of information; you must decide the most effective ways to furnish it.

How do you discuss a problem with a client? At many points in the project there are problems that you cannot fix or cover. There are times when a client must make a decision on a problem issue, an issue they are not going to be happy about. Don't tell them about the problem until you have a solution or two. If you tell clients about the problem too soon, they may make it larger because they probably don't understand that they have options. Wait until you can offer a solution before telling the client of a problem. Explain the problem and present your recommendations at the same time, always giving options and explaining your own choice. When you do so, say, "We understand that there may be information that we don't have, which may affect the solution you choose."

Then the clients go home feeling they have an answer, a choice, and not a problem. You must consider your legal liabilities, but it is still best to use this approach.

During the past decade, when the economy had a negative influence on many areas, the designers who stayed very close to their clients had a better chance of maintaining their client base. Very often those firms which stayed close to their clients were small design studios. Staying close meant their clients saw them as part of their team. People buy from people . . . they don't buy from organizations.

And interior design is based on personal relationships. Develop that rapport with your clients using these procedures and others you may have discovered on your own. If you want to keep the client and stay out of court, you need to maintain a relationship that constantly supports the client. They need to feel that you are part of their team. As long as they feel that they are important, they are not likely to sue you and they are more likely to refer that next project to you.

Treat your contractors and your suppliers the way you would treat your clients, and they will become team members in selling projects to your clients. This can do a great deal to build rapport. One of the main things that designers need in order to produce the proper job today is the right quality of vendors and contractors behind us. With good vendors, designers can supply their clients with many things that would not otherwise be available. Building this team, and this rapport, is critical for a good marketing practice in this next decade.

Give recognition for jobs well done. When a contractor or member of your staff is working well on a project, take a minute to give that positive reinforcement, as Spencer Johnson and Ken Blanchard suggest in *The One Minute Manager*. Go out of your way to compliment the deserving person, but find a specific task that has been done and compliment it specifically. This means more than general compliments.

Chapter **15**

Organization

Organizing is a necessary part of selling, just as it is part of every other thing we do. The interior design discipline is based on organization. The NCIDQ test, which evaluates interior designers and qualifies them, is based strongly on our ability to organize. A designer must complete an accredited design program before being qualified for the exam.

A selling presentation, or any other type of marketing program, must be organized. It must have structure. Large corporations invest a great deal of time training their salespeople in the organizational process of selling, to ensure that the total process, step-by-step, is adequately covered. Some programs feature nine steps, others have ten or twelve. This varies, but there is consistent order to the presentation structure.

Prepare a list with an organizational format of every topic that needs to be covered in the meeting with your client. Without it, you're more likely to miss things. You'll come back without certain information because you have not reviewed their thinking thoroughly. You have not checked with them to make sure that the foundation is secure before going on to the next level.

Before you schedule a meeting, make sure you have your checklist ready. With that checklist, you'll not only make sure that you cover everything, but you'll appear far more professional because you know that every item there will be covered; you'll also be sure that the meeting will be very successfully presented.

Sometimes we work on a design for weeks or months; of course we understand it and are comfortable with it. But the client may not have such a clear understanding. We owe them a carefully planned orientation if we expect them to buy into our plan.

Take the preparation time to not only review objectives but to consider all personal information previously gathered, such as the decision making process, areas of comfort and experience, and their approach. The more you can tie together a client's preferences with your decisions and plan, the easier it is for the client to understand and accept.

Too often, meetings are arranged to meet the expected schedule without allowing the proper preparation time, not only for generating and reviewing design materials, but also for considering the many different demands for communication style. This client is different. In fact, may be *very* different from the client you met at the previous meeting. You must shift gears and be ready for the client's style.

Communication is the key to a client buying your design. So design your approach to clients as carefully as you do any part of your design project.

The forms we suggest are designed to force us to plan and organize meetings in a way which builds strong positive relationships and which help us accomplish our objectives.

You will find that if you use a meeting plan guide (Figure 15-1) as a base for your meetings, you will think and act in a more directed manner.

For the meeting, make yourself a list that covers items to be discussed, with space where you can note the results as the meeting progresses.

SET PRIORITIES

The purpose of this documentation is to force us to see the priorities. Sometimes ours are different from our clients'. Many of us have spent endless hours developing a part of a project that has no value or interest to the client, even though we think it is the most important part.

Decide what is important to you and spend your time on that, otherwise you can end up wasting too much project time on something that is really not relevant to the project. Look at that time schedule. How does this fit with the priorities? Is it really worth it?

When you take on a client, one of the first things you need to do is to find out how the client will handle a given problem. How do they deal with problems? It's a good idea to review different issues with them and to see what is important, and what they are willing to spend money on. This is part of your interviewing technique and it's worth repeating throughout the job. Be sure you know what their value system is.

SYNOPSIS

Before going to any client meeting—either in person or on the phone:

- Review previous and existing knowledge of the project.
- Be sure there is a reason for this appointment. Yes, it's good to spend time with clients to get to know them, but as

professionals we need to be sure we use every minute effectively.

- Outline the goals and objectives for the meeting, including those that the clients perhaps generated in a past meeting or by phone. Yours may be similar to the client's . . . the result of a client's question. Or your expectations as the designer and orchestrator of the project may surpass the client's expectations. If this is the case, a carefully planned map is needed to make this transition comfortable and understandable for the client. (Refer to Figures 15-1 through 15-5.)

MEETING PLANNING GUIDE

Client Name: Date:

Current Situation:

Problems or Needs:

Goals and Objectives:

    Overall:

    This Meeting:

Questions That Need To Be Answered:

    Client's

    Designer's

What information, etc., will client need in order to make a decision?

What *values* are we offering

How can our firm provide the best *benefits* to this client?

What *questions* can we expect to ask the client?

What are the best *answers* to these questions?

What are the *commitments* does the client need to make at this time?

Considering the situation, how will I measure the *accomplishments* of this meeting?

Figure 15-1

Client Meeting

Client Name: _____ Date: _____

Objectives	Results
Client Objectives:	
Designers Objectives:	
Questions:	

© *Design Business Monthly*

Figure 15-2

Results of Client Meeting

Client Name: _____ Date: _____

Items Incomplete:

Needs:

Research and Information Required:

Date and Method of Next Contact:

Figure 15-3

Value Worksheet

Proposed Design Features	Purpose or Benefit	Support Information

Figure 15-4

```
                                                                    1
Part II Form:

Client Meeting Debriefing Summary

1. Specific Interest


2. Communication methods that resulted in positive response:


3. Techniques used:                        Results:


4. My feelings


5a. Decision Style


5b. What's important:


6. Client's knowledge, thoughts, feelings about our firm,
our approach:


7. Is this client similar to other clients?


8. What other things have I learned?


9. In which ways did I perform well?

10. What areas deserve improvement?
```

Figure 15-5

Chapter 16

The Art of the Interview

The art of listening makes the difference between a good relationship with clients and one full of problems and misunderstandings. To be a good listener, show that you are committed to the conversation. If you are interested in what your clients are saying, look at them. Maintaining eye contact is essential, because some people feel that when you aren't looking at them you aren't paying attention. At the very least, your looking away is distracting. Do not participate in any other kind of activity during this conversation, but dedicate your interest to them.

Secondly, give them feedback. Let the speakers know that you are concentrating as you listen. Say, "Yes, I understand." Or you may even ask a question that supports or develops particular points of what they are talking about. If you interrupt, do it politely to bring out points of interest that might clarify the issue.

Handle distractions and interruptions discreetly. If something happens to distract you, deal with it but come back as quickly as possible. The client must know that you are dedicated to their conversation and to what they have to say.

Take notes. They can be short and abbreviated, but write down enough so that you understand what has been said when you reread them. After the conversation, review the notes with the client. Say, "This is a summary of what I think we covered here. I'd like to go over them with you to make sure it's correct, so that when I go back to my office I'll know where to start." (Figure 15-2 is an outline that you might use.)

Sometimes you may want to tape a conversation. If you do so, still summarize the conversation with the client at the end to make sure all points are covered. Tell whoever types up these notes to work only from that end portion of the tape, which clarifies your discussions. You have listed all the issues, you've reviewed them with the client, and you have gone through the decision-making process. Making a printed transcript of a total conversation is really time-consuming, and it is much more difficult to locate any information you need in a bulky transcript. Often, things change during a conversation. It is much better to have just the summarized format.

Emotion can be confusing, and clients do get emotional over their spaces. Sometimes when clients are very angry, they will say things that are almost impossible to understand and which may be taken incorrectly. This is another time when it is very good to say, "Now let me summarize exactly what you said." At that point, you may even ask them to tape a summary of the clarification. This also works well with phone calls.

When you walk into a client's house, go with the attitude that you are there to learn and to listen. Even though you are trying to evaluate the situation, be careful not to go in with a judgmental attitude. Listen first. Let the clients tell you what they want to say. After you've absorbed their information, then you can deal with your opinion. But listen with the attitude of "I am here to understand what you are saying" or "I'm evaluating the situation carefully before I will consider passing judgement".

Evaluating a situation too quickly can be dangerous. Some situations take years to develop. Often the easy-to-see situations can be evaluated quickly. After all, you've been doing this for years. You know how things work. But the client thinks his situation is unique. He thinks it is serious; after all, it is not worth paying a consultant for a common problem.

Do not assume that the client really wants your advice. After you have summarized the situation with the client, then ask, "Exactly which issues did you want us to help you with?" It may be that they really are not interested in your working on certain issues, even though they may appear to be disturbed about them. They may not be ready to handle those situations.

It is best to let them explain the project to you. Afterwards, review it with them. You may wish to say, "The way you've explained it, these are the issues that I think you want addressed. Is this correct? Let's go over these carefully and let's decide whether this really is what you want to address first." Allow the client to set the priorities.

Watch for visual clues. Very often, the posture of a client, the way they may move or the way they appear to be uncomfortable about certain issues, may tell you something about what that client really feels but is afraid to share with you. Sometimes we use very different words to describe our thoughts, and often that body language will give us a clue about their real meaning.

As we listen to our clients, often we don't understand what they're saying, or maybe it doesn't relate to what we're doing. Ask them to explain.

- Could you explain more about _____ ?
- That's very interesting. Tell me a bit more about it.
- What do you feel is the most important part of this space?
- Could you explain more about how you use this space?
- What type of space would be more comfortable for your situation?
- What would make this room work better in view of your changed situation?

Listen carefully. Before going onto the next question, restate to the client what you think was said. Then explain how this may influence the design direction. Very often in hearing your version and what it will entail, clients will realize that what they said may not be what they actually wanted. Rather than saying up front, "You're wrong," it's often better to go back and explain. "Are you sure this is what you want to happen?" is a safe question.

We are constantly communicating, but the question is how adequately and how effectively and how articulately. One thing most of us learn is that the more time we give a client to talk, the better they feel we are presented. Some of the best presenters I've seen are those who did really very little talking. They are the ones who let the clients talk; they let the clients explain their objectives and missions. They make the client feel important. We are not selling; we are building longterm relationships. We are building rapport. Developing relationships and rapport is a positive, pleasurable experience for the client.

Think about past presentations, what went well and what didn't. Try to figure out why some things worked and some failed because you have to do everything possible to make the designer/client relationship a special one for our clients.

1. Be sure you know what the client really wants. What are their real concerns? Ask questions. Sometimes the "calling cards," the reason the client says he or she is calling a designer, are not the real concern.
2. Take time. This relationship-building experience requires care and time.
3. Don't rush to answer the question. Wait a minute. Leave a few seconds of silence. Make it appear that you are considering their question seriously before answering.
4. Answer their concerns in a caring manner. Show your professionalism. Don't condescend.
5. Review all points discussed to be sure you are all going in the same direction. It's often necessary to review and consolidate different comments to be sure the parties understand one another. Sometimes these change in the course of the interview. I find it's best to be prepared to treat people as if they were very important.

VERBAL FINESSE

Sometimes it isn't what you say, but how you say it. First of all, let the clients know that you are committed to them. Don't just say you'll see that X gets done; set a date and a time and make a commitment to do it. If you have agreed to have it completed by Tuesday, see that it is done before then.

When you disagree with clients, you can risk alienating them by saying so directly. It is better to say that there are several ways to handle the issue. Tell them you will try your best to understand their viewpoint, but in return could they consider yours. Perhaps you, the design firm, have misinterpreted their viewpoint. Your plan was not done casually; you must have missed something.

Because their viewpoint has not been rejected out of hand; they will be more willing to contemplate an alternative method. You, as the person put into the decision making process, must make the final decision. Once you have explained your position, perhaps the client can concede graciously. Or the client may explain that because of other aspects of the situation, the decision must change direction. There are priorities that their institution considers much greater and these must take precedence.

The more research you do in advance, the less likely this is to happen.

Do your best to prevent clients from making costly mistakes. If you know their decision is wrong, put off acting on it. Give them more information so that they can make informed decisions.

Don't blame the client for making the wrong decision or handling it incorrectly. It is probably your fault for not presenting the situation properly. It can help to say to the client, "I feel I haven't presented this properly. I believe that we are putting the project in jeopardy if we do not make the decision this way. Here are the reasons." Take the blame yourself rather than saying that a client lacks knowledge, or has done something wrong.

When a client asks for something, nothing is impossible. Everything can be done, but can it be done within reason, within price constraints and without taking excessive amounts of time? You may want to safeguard yourself by telling the client, "Let me get you the estimates on this because I have a feeling that this may be far more expensive than we expected. When we get the costs, you will be better able to make the decision of whether you want to make the investment."

Ask your clients what they want and need. Make it easy for them to tell you by asking them if they would be willing to act as unpaid consultants in helping you improve your services. Are there two or three things that they can suggest you do to improve your firm?

Instead of asking clients if they are happy with the project, ask if there is any way you could improve it or give them better service next time. What is important to the client? Enlist their help in seeing things from a client's perspective.

Be honest with your clients. If time is an issue, tell them you have a time problem now and must leave to work on something else. Let them know that you have a problem, and that you will get back to them when you can.

The best way to learn about a client is through the Socratic method: ask questions. Then listen carefully, speak occasionally, observe, question, and probe. The way you ask questions affects the answers you get. Don't always offer an opinion or make a judgement. Try to be neutral. Don't agree or disagree, but carefully listen to what is being said.

Use nonverbal probes: smile or nod and watch the body language of your clients.

Try short verbal probes: Yes, Sure, Right, Of course. How do you feel? What do you think of that?

Use echo probes: repeat what the client says in order to encourage him or her to enlarge on the topic.

One of the most difficult things we learn as designers is when to stop talking. When you interview clients, let them talk. There is a way to present your issues professionally, while allowing your clients to express their thoughts. The format for the design service outline is effective because you are reviewing the different services of the firm while asking about a client's needs.

See if you can work on developing those particular clients and find ways to make them comfortable in presenting to you—not just listening to you presenting to them. Can they reveal their needs, express their problems? Is this done in a cooperative manner?

The ability to give clients what they want is a big part of selling, and you cannot do it without the help and support of your staff. Enlist their cooperation. Instead of announcing that the firm has a deadline that must be met or you'll all be in trouble, you could say "We have a challenge here. We have a client who has a need and if we can please this client, I know it will lead to additional work. In your opinion, what can be done to assure that this is completed on time?"

SAMPLE INTERVIEW

For a business client:

Q. How long have you been in this space?

A. About seven years. We didn't plan to be here this long, but the rent is reasonable and moving seems too complex. The neighborhood is good and clients know where we are. I know the building isn't perfect, but we have learned to work with the problems. But we must have more space.

(You have learned more than you asked. People generally will give you their reasons for doing or not doing things.)

Q. You mentioned that you were considering adding space across the hall, rather than moving to a new location. Is this a good location for you?

A. Reasonably. It is convenient to where we live and to our clients. Most of our sources are nearby.

Q. How many of your clients visit the office?

A. About 80 percent.

Q. What are the reasons?

A. They come in to consult on how our services are working for their firms, and to see our new, state-of-the-art equipment.

Q. And your clients are involved in what types of businesses?

A. Normally businesses with fifty to three thousand employees, directed to sales, marketing, and distribution.

(This indicates the type of business it is. Continue along these lines to learn more about the company and the way it works. You will find that this puts the client at ease. Ask them more about their clients' needs, how much time they spend in the office, the size of their projects, and the number of years of service. What is their sales approach? Throughout the interview, draw them out to learn their backgrounds, the artistic styles, and detailing that appeal to them, etc.)
For a residential client:

Q. How long have you lived here?

A. Twelve years.

Q. It looks like a great neighborhood.

A. It is great for the kids and that is one reason we want to stay here. If it were just my husband and me, we'd probably build our dream house on a mountain. Chauffeuring the kids to social activities every day is more than I want to deal with at this point. Besides, this is close to where my husband works. If we were farther away, I'd never see him.

(This answered my unstated question of why they sought interior design services. The house was in a nice neighborhood but not in the exclusive area I would have expected, based on his position and expected income. Some of the client's plans seemed too extravagant for the quality of the house, but their reasons for staying there, their desire for personal convenience, and the social activities of their children, make the investment worthwhile for them. They can well afford the budget. So why shouldn't they have some of the conveniences that others in the same social position enjoy? They put a high value on family life and want to encourage the family to make its home the base for much of its activity.)

These are simplistic short interviews, just to show the technique of asking leading questions. The point is that you must see their building as being *valuable* to them. It is a space with emotions, memories, and history. It is a part of them. A designer must see how these intangibles fit within the rationale of the project.

Chapter 17

Your Corporate Image

What do you want your clients to think about your firm? What is your position in the industry? How are you seen in relation to your competition?

We want to be responsible for designing our own corporate images. Every designer likes to feel that he or she is in control, but sometimes we don't understand exactly what it is that we are supposed to control.

Your corporate image can be formed by people outside your firm and even by your competitors. You may need to seek the advice of outside consultants for an objective viewpoint of your firm and its image. You may know your company's strengths and weaknesses, but are they being suitably conveyed to the outside world?

Your corporate image is made up not only from graphics and logos, but comes from all of the components that make up your particular practice. How do you want to be perceived? What is the future direction of your firm? And how do you want to be positioned in the next few years?

Corporate image requires constant attention. Interior design is a business built on change. As the trends in the field change, so does our work and so should our corporate images. Although style is important, it isn't the sole element of a strong corporate image. It is essential to retain some consistency so that the image serves to represent your firm professionally.

In this area we need a high-level graphic design expert, someone who understands the discipline the way we understand ours.

DRESS

In design we need to look the part. Clients expect a certain quality of presentation. It is usually advisable to dress in a business-like fashion, although clients do like to see designers working and they understand that we need clothing that permits us to get into action at times. Don't fall into the trap of thinking you must dress as well as your clients. In most instances their income is considerably higher than ours. However, we still can dress wtih style.

If clothes sense is not one of your strong points, enlist the help of a fashion consultant to show you how to style your wardrobe so that it really projects the appropriate image. There are many books, including *Dress for Success* by John Malloy, and a number of others, which have underscored the importance of the appropriate dress for business.

Even if you are very style-conscious, perhaps you should hire an image consultant to review your style and see if you are projecting the image you want to project. It's interesting to hear a new point of view, and it's hard to be objective about yourself.

ENVIRONMENT

Your office should give a good first impression of your firm. It should be clean and provide for the client's comfort. It is important to be able to offer them even a limited menu of refreshments—at least good drinking water—and clean restrooms. After all, if you're going to have a long meeting, the restrooms become a very necessary part of the day. So take the time to be extra sure that these matters meet the standards with which you want your clients to associate you.

Is your studio a good example of your work? You deserve to look well in your space, and you deserve a space that is easy to work in. Some well-published designers live and work in spaces that don't represent their work. A good studio need not be expensive, but it must be well-designed.

How can you sell interior design when you don't practice what you preach?

BUSINESS ETIQUETTE

Good business etiquette contributes to your company's image. Keeping in touch with your clients is an important part of a good marketing program. It is important to acknowledge and respond to all invitations, even if you are not interested in attending. Simply drop a note and say you can't attend, and that you will continue to give your personal support—or some nice personal touch.

When you are entertained, send a thank you note. Send it in writing so that it stays in their files, even though you might make a phone call to thank the person, too.

Be sensitive to the expectations of others. Be sure to return phone calls or ensure that there is some appropriate response made at the correct time: usually immediately.

Good manners are often taken for granted, but today we see article after article in business magazines on business etiquette. It's very sad to realize that we have a whole generation of executives who need remedial training in etiquette. Among the people we work with, it is crucial to show general courtesies and appropriate manners. It is really important to be basically kind and nice to people.

If you find that you're not able to show these courtesies because you're in a bad mood or have had problems, stay away from the clients. There are some days that many people just don't belong near people, let alone clients. You can't afford to let this part of your personality show, so keep it hidden and find ways to monitor and moderate your personal style so that you at least seem to be a positive, nice person.

I have met designers who are excellent designers at their work but who have few social skills. It may be that they lack patience in developing relationships with clients. If this sounds like you, then perhaps you need to find someone who will work with you to deal with the clients on a day-to-day basis, and do the hand-holding and the nurturing that is necessary for developing and nurturing your business.

All of us have times when we are overwrought or burned out because of many of the things that occur in our general practices. Find some form of recreation that restores your good spirits.

Teach your craftspeople, and all of the people who are working around clients, to be really polite and talk with the clients in an appropriate fashion. Teach them to explain to the clients those parts of the job and its processes that are important to them. If, however, there are questions or changes desired, then it is most important that anyone working on the project direct it back to the design office; after all they may not be aware of all the issues that are involved and, therefore, the decisions made may be inappropriate.

So let those clients know how you do things, what you do, and the reason, and then they will become better clients.

How does your voice sound on the telephone? Is it weak and hesitant? Do you sound disorganized? Or are you firm and strong? Do you make a good impression? These are points that

George R. Walther is considered one of the leaders in effective telephone procedures. He has many rules; here is a mixture of some of his with others added:

1. Always be the one to make the call.
2. Never just make the call. Plan first. It often takes an hour or more to do this preparation.
3. Clear your desk of other unrelated items and have everything related to the issue ready. Go over the material. Check issues with your staff before starting so that you are ready for any questions.
4. Be sure you will not be interrupted. He likes to walk around the room using a hand set. I like to work with a regular phone so I am sure the client can hear my best voice.
5. Start by building rapport.
6. Carefully outline the items to be covered. Be sure they are in an easy to understand order. Make a list of issues on a pad:

Questions   Answers

so you can be sure all the issues are covered.

you can easily test by taping your phone calls. There's a small gadget available from almost any telephone supply store for that purpose. Simply attach it to your phone and you can tape telephone conversations. I also use it for taping details of telephone meetings.

TELEPHONE

The telephone is a machine that can work for you or against you. Like any other tool, its use requires management skills.

It can save you time, yet still there will be days when you wish it had never been invented because dealing with calls has eaten up your day.

Accept the telephone as a convenience and an opportunity to meet people rather than seeing it as a bother, an annoyance, or a time-waster. The person on the other end of the phone can tell what your attitude is when you pick up the phone. If you're not in the mood to talk to people, arrange for someone else in your studio to take the calls. You can return them when you're in a better mood.

When you're on the telephone, usually you need to speak more slowly than you do in normal conversations. Normal conversation is around 150 words a minute. If you can reduce this to about one hundred words a minute, it really enhances communication. After all, the person is not sitting across from you . . . you cannot tell through their body language whether you are being understood. So try speaking a little slower and, from time to time, ask a question to test whether they do understand the issues you've been presenting. Just check the facts.

It is important to let the other person know that you know who they are; use their name. If you're not sure that they know exactly who you are, give them some references. Tell them where you met; mention people you know in common. Make sure that they can put you in context with the issue under discussion. Otherwise, there is no point in continuing the conversation.

Sometimes you'll get a caller who says only, "This is David." That's terrific! You only know about nine hundred Davids, so which one is it? You can end up putting clients on hold while listening to "David" in a fog.

Give the other person the benefit of the doubt. When you call, clearly identify yourself. Say you are calling regarding X, which the two of you discussed previously. Then ask if it is a convenient time to talk about it. Just because the phone rings doesn't mean it's a convenient time for the client. And if it isn't a convenient time, ask when you should call back.

I believe in telephone appointments. If I tell a client or supplier that we will talk again on Thursday, I also suggest a time, for instance between 8:30 and 9 o'clock, and ask if that is convenient. Once the time is agreed on, I write it in my appointment book with any other appointment for that day.

Before starting a phone call, write out an agenda using the meeting form, just as you would for any other meeting. Make a list of everything that you want to cover in that particular phone call. Let the recipient know what the agenda is ahead of time, so that if they need a file or if they need to refer to another person for information, they will have time to prepare.

At the end of the call, summarize what was discussed. This means that when you pick up the telephone, you must have a notepad in front of you, as well as the client's file and any other information that pertains to the subject. When you're concluding the call, ask if they mind if you put on your tape recorder and tape the summary as you go through it with them. Then, when you reread your notes, is the perfect time for them to correct any mistaken impressions or add any other items they think should be brought out. And very often people do remember additional details they would like covered.

Have the tape transcribed immediately, and send a copy to the client. Keep another copy for your files, and do anything you said you would do. Always follow the call with a letter.

In summary, consider a phone call to be a meeting. Schedule it with equal care and concern for the person you are calling, especially if it is a call early in the relationship. Your professionalism must shine through. Respect the client's time.

COMMON COURTESIES

Focus your attention on the caller. You can't be doing four things—eating breakfast, talking on the telephone, taking notes, and watching television—it doesn't work. Be focussed, get to the point, and try not to interrupt.

Have patience. Sometimes people speak so slowly that it seems they go on forever! It may be entirely possible to say in one sentence what it's taken them a half hour to explain. But they think it's important. They want to explain it to you. So you must have patience and listen to them. Don't interrupt people. Understand that when you're speaking on the phone, you must have good posture, you must have a good disposition, you must be ready for that phone call. Many times I will stand during a phone call because it gives me better posture and I feel that I sound better.

Try to be positive in your phone calls. Eliminate negative phrases from your vocabulary. When you're talking with a client, speak about a subject that you can be sure of. Don't hedge. It's better to say, "I don't know the scheduling. I'll call you back tomorrow morning and give you the schedule." Allow yourself enough time. Schedule a time for a return call. Promise action, and then make sure that action is carried out.

I know there are many one-upsmanship techniques, but I'm not comfortable in that sort of relationship. I believe we must make every effort to present ourselves as professionals if we are to expect the right outcome in a relationship. I believe in being truthful. I try to tell clients just what the story is, but I don't tell them about a problem until I have a solution. A few years ago, a contractor who was managing a large project for which we were providing interior design services would, together with the person who was managing the project, call the client to explain all the problems. She followed her call to the client with a call to me. I'd ask for a solution; she would say she didn't know but would have answers the next day. Finally, I suggested that she wait to call the client until she had some options.

Who should answer your telephone? It should be the person who knows the most about your company, not the person you hired last week. A properly trained telephone receptionist can save you and your staff more time than anyone on your payroll. They can separate the calls that you must handle from the ones on which they can check information and call back.

Try to answer the phone within two or three rings, if possible. Try to answer phones promptly, even if you must say to someone, "Excuse me a moment, I'm on the other line. Would you hold for a moment?"

Answering machines are useful. I'm delighted when people have an answering machine, because it provides a way to leave a message. When I leave messages, I try to be specific about the reason for calling, whether it is details of carpet selection, or whether I need prices. I try to give them enough information that when they return my call, they'll have the answers. I don't have to sit and wait on the phone while they dig up information for the proper answers. Leave good messages, whether with a person or whether on an answering machine. Ask any staffers who take messages to be precise, even to the point of reading back the message to the callers. Make sure that they know how to spell that client's name and they know the correct telephone number. Transposing just one number can cost you time. Suppose there are forty-seven David Wilsons in the phone book!

Check telephone numbers. Check name spellings. Make sure that you know why the person called.

Do you like playing phone tag? This annoying occurrence can be avoided by scheduling calls. All you have to do is say, "I'm sorry that I can't speak with you at the moment, if you would be kind enough to call again sometime after 4 o'clock today, I expect to be back in my ofice." You can leave the message on an answering machine, or ask the person who mans the phones to say it.

Remember that the caller has taken time out of his or her schedule and that it's a priority for them.

Mobile phones and cellular phones have saved a lot of time, but they are not completely private, so be careful. Mobile phones are useful in staying in touch with your offices and for personal calls if you are on the road a lot. They can be expensive. At one point, it cost $40 per month for our mobile phone charges; today it's costing between $300 and $400 per month for the same number of calls and the same service.

Conference calls can be confusing. When you're making a conference call, make sure that the person at the other end is aware of everyone else involved in the conference call. A chairperson should identify each person by name and function: this person happens to be in charge of production in the factory; another handles scheduling, pricing, and whatever else is involved.

Can everyone hear clearly? Some of our services are not as clear as they should be. Conference calls are worthwhile but they must be correctly programmed, otherwise they can cause total chaos and great confusion.

The telephone will be with us for a long time. You can save 50 percent of your time on the phone each week, just by organizing your phonetime properly. It's impossible to run a business without phones, so use them properly. Make sure that everyone in your firm knows the etiquette, studies the procedures, and tests them out periodically by recording the phone calls. Make sure you know how each of your staff sounds to the client.

Chapter **18**

Pre-Selling

In order to have clients, you must first have prospects. You can do beautiful design work. You can offer a great specialty. But if there is no client out there who needs and wants your services, you're not going to have any work. It is unfortunate, but in most cases too much of our education is dedicated to developing great design. It often seems that no one considers the client's needs or the budget; we're not even told to consider budgets. In many instances, designers who graduate from design school have never seen a real client. We must find ourselves a situation where we have prospects who have a need.

Keep a record of everything you do; make a file for each new potential client. If a prospect is important enough to approach, you need a good record. In addition to the standard information you need to generate, include a general client contact summary with the client's name, source of the referral, and the contacts you have made. Note each contact by date and type: was it a telephone call, a form letter, a personally directed letter, brochure, visit, or a meeting through social opportunity? This will be kept in the front of the file.

To generate business, you must first market your firm in a way that defines its positions for potential clients. This creates a desire for what we offer. Then you must, by building that relationship or selling, transform that desire into a transaction. You must provide service to that client in a way that builds an ongoing relationship throughout the project, through the follow-up and everything the design firm does.

If at any point in the project the design firm fails to maintain that strong service relationship, it can destroy everything else the firm has done. That is because we have allowed the client to know us, and people who know us can do us harm. Once you have decided to take on the client, you must be prepared to build that continuing relationship because that is what makes a designer's career.

Does the client have the ability to buy? In many instances, clients just cannot afford what we want to do for them, or they don't hold the company position that would permit them to make decisions about our product. It is important to find the right person and to be sure all efforts are directed to that person. If the clients do not have the desire and need to buy what we want, the relationship you build will not immediately provide you with the business you desire. It is very difficult to define and find the "best" clients and to support them appropriately.

Today we must learn to be directed and to look for clients who are *right* for your firm. If you have a prospect, how do you get the opportunity to make a presentation?

EMISSARY METHOD OF SELLING

Using an emissary is an excellent way to develop a market. Firms often hire a person to act as an emissary. This person will pre-interview prospective clients. He or she will size up the project and its general qualifications. He or she will present the design firm in glowing detail, telling the potential client about the principals in charge, the design staff and the management group. Then this person sets up a time for a formal presentation, at which he or she is also present.

By the time of the presentation, the emissary will have developed a friendship with the prospective client. An emissary will assist in the communication between the client and the design team, and will bring business to a firm. But he or she will continue to look out for the interests of the prospective clients he or she has developed.

INTRODUCTORY CALLS

If you don't have business, there is a way of getting it, and that is through cold calls. Professional marketers tell us that if you have no work at all, and you really want to develop a firm, there is no question that this is the way to do it.

There are design firms today that have as many as fifty or sixty people doing nothing but making cold calls. In the contract field there are not too many repeat clients; basically most of the jobs come from new people. If that is the case, then cold calling makes a lot of sense for this market.

A specialist in cold calls told me he makes fifteen cold calls per day. He reaches seven people, and from them he makes one appointment. For every five people he sees, he makes one sale. This results in fifty sales per year.

He has a list of what qualifies a customer, and goes through it on each call. He determines exactly how to qualify the client, how to obtain the information he needs, how to build the appropriate rapport, and then how to close the sale. He knows that if he skips any of the issues, he is not going to accomplish that sale. He is also aware that if he makes cold calls on a continuing basis, he will continue to have business. And this is what keeps him going when people don't qualify, are rude, and worse. Action brings results.

Professional salespeople spend about 45 percent of their time prospecting; 20 percent of their time presenting; 20 percent of their time demonstrating product knowledge; and at least 15 to 20 percent of their time in personal development and education to make sure that they are ready to be good salespeople.

As design firms, we need to look at the amount of lead time from prospect to the final sale. This runs, ordinarily, somewhere from four weeks to three years, depending upon the type of project. This means that not only do you have to maintain regular contact with your prospective clients, but that you must prospect constantly to keep your studio as busy as you want it to be. You also have to realize that if you don't do some prospecting and developing today, you are unlikely to have the business four months from now, or two or three years from now.

So many design publications are presenting selling as if it were a battle, and I'm not sure they are wrong. They tell us first, that we need excellent training to go to war. Sales are not made strictly by chance; they are made by people who spend a lot of time training and working and developing their particular expertise, not just in design, but also in their presentation skills. Just as in war, we also have a very strong opponent. Somebody else is after that job; you are not the only firm. Therefore, it is a question of who will win the job. Maybe we need to consider our sales development more like the battles of war.

To build a strong sales list, you need to spend thirty to forty minutes a day prospecting, making cold calls. Then you are likely to have a continuing flow of new clients. Schedule your work so you can meet a few clients each week. For cold calling to work well you must make it part of your routine. To develop your prospect list, read the local papers for news of new buildings, weddings, divorces, mergers and acquisitions, and partnership announcements.

In any cold call, first you must get a prospect's attention. A sample script is: "Good morning, (Name), this is (your name) from (your firm's name). I've read (or heard) that you are moving to a new building. We are a design firm that can work with you on this type of project. I called to schedule an appointment to tell you more of what we can do for you. Are you available Wednesday afternoon at 4 o'clock?".

If at this point the prospect says, "I'm not interested," you ask why. If they are too busy, ask if there is a better time. If they really don't want to hear from you at all, ask if they could tell you why. The roadblock could be financial. Or they may say that they have someone else.

You can still turn it around by saying, "It has been interesting to me to see how many businesses like yours have ended up using our services after considering other people. I am going to send you a brochure on our firm. Will you just keep us in mind? If your design firm doesn't work out, let us know. Do you mind if I call you back in a month or so to see just what develops?"

If they say, "I'll call you back," you should respond with, "Would you mind if I called you tomorrow morning at 10 to see how your schedule is going?"

If they suggest that you send them the material instead of making an appointment, tell them you really prefer not to mail information because many of the projects you do are very individual. It would be beneficial to both of you to meet in person. Is there a time that he or she can give you just a few minutes so that you can explain exactly how you can help *them*?

Or, after considering all the other objections, you may say that many clients who initially said they weren't interested changed their minds once they saw the design program. Then you might say, "If you have a few moments, I would be delighted to have one of our specialists stop and talk with you, or I would be happy to talk with you."

The point is, cold calling is a question of verbal salesmanship. The battle is to get a prospect going in your direction so that you have the opportunity to meet with them in person. That person-to-person interaction should be your goal.

When making cold calls, do it in front of a mirror so that you can watch yourself. When we act and look enthusiastic, it shows on the other end of the phone. Keep a timer so then you know exactly how long you are talking. Generally, a cold call should take three minutes. Keep track of the forty-five minutes a day you set aside for cold calling and see how many people you can reach within that time. Keep a record of each call and of any problem areas. Find yourself a consultant and talk to him or her about these problem areas. Perhaps he or she can give you a few tips and some verbal terminology that might help you be more successful in your next calls.

Practice. You need to practice before you pick up the telephone. Know exactly what you are going to say and have your outline in front of you so that you are sure to hit all the important points. It may help to stand up when you speak on the telephone. If you are standing and can watch yourself, your animation increases and you sound much more interesting. Just remember, that client cannot see you—they can only hear you. Therefore, every bit of expression and animation helps.

To be a good salesperson, you must have ability and skill. You need to know how to communicate in the sales field. This means that you need good people skills as well as good sales skills, and an appropriate schedule for carrying them out. Secondly, you must be committed to producing and you must be persistent.

Persistence wins clients. An art specialist from a gallery with a mediocre line has sold many exceptional projects due to persistence. He followed up each appointment with faxed information that day. The next day the prospect received a hand-delivered information packet about the meeting. There was information forthcoming on a constant basis, so there was no way his prospects could forget about him. And in many respects, that consistency is really what brought forward the sales.

A primary reason for making introductory or development calls is to keep your name in front of the clients. This can be done for any reason at all. If you can think of any reason to call them, do so. Send press releases on completed projects or special events you have planned. Send them birthday cards or congratulations—anything that is appropriate. Just keep your name in front of that client who has a special need.

SALES LETTERS

Sales letters are an inexpensive, personal, and direct way to put your message in front of a prospect. There is a technique to writing good sales letters. You don't have to be a master wordsmith. If you follow these guidelines, you should be able to produce an effective sales letter.

Use the first sentence to entice the prospects. Tests show that people are most likely to read the first sentence and the postscript. Repeat the same point in different ways during the letter in order to reinforce that point.

Keep the letter simple and well-written. Your prospect will notice errors or imperfections. Be personable. Write it as if you were talking to them and be careful to feature facts, not exaggerated exclamations. This letter represents your firm.

This type of writing is different from other types of editorial work. It must be dedicated to four specific issues.

First, you must show how the client will benefit. Your prospects will be interested in this letter only if they get something out of it. Before you write the letter, you should have done some market research to pinpoint the client. You need to know something about this client's situation so that you can relate your specialty to their need.

Second, explain the benefits. Be specific. Don't say you have a great service; show it by specific example.
For example:

- We offer you a design service that is dedicated to increasing productivity within the office environment.
- Our firm will help you with your space planning. It will also manage the procurement of needed furnishings.

Third, present your credentials: the age of your business, professional affiliations, educational background, and other experiences that would support your credentials.

Finally, encourage the client to take some action. Present a benefit of calling for immediate action. Encourage them to call you because you have a particular offering that is important to them. Or better yet, write that you will call them at an appointed time.

Client Contact Summary

Client Name: _____

Address: _____

Telephone Number(s): _____

Source of Referral: _____

_____

Date	Form	Result	Follow-Up

Examples: B - Brochure, PC - Phone Call, LI - Letter of Interest, SM - Social Meeting

© *Design Business Monthly*

Figure 18-1

Weekly Sales Sheet

Number of Prospects Called:

Contacts with decisions makers:

Appointments set:

       made:

Presentation Made:

New Clients Obtained:

Referrals:

Leads:

© *Design Business Monthly*

Figure 18-2

Chapter 19

The Presentation

The best place to make a formal presentation to a client is on your turf, if you can manage it and if you have a well-designed studio. It's always better to make a presentation on your turf because you are in control.

This isn't always possible, especially when you are interviewing for a large project and you are one of many firms making presentations. In this instance, you either want to be first or last. Last is typically the best, and first is usually the next best. The middle is the weakest position. Check the scheduling in advance. If at all possible, position yourself to advantage.

How many people should you bring to that presentation? It depends on the number of people to whom you will be making the presentation. If there are twelve people, your contingent may number five or six. They should include the principal of the firm, if your firm is large. The principal introduces the project manager and other staff who will work on the project. After the presentation, both the project manager and the principal answer questions. If the presentation is held in the design studio, you may give the prospects a tour of the office. A tour of similar projects may be suggested.

The amount of time the prospective client allows you for the presentation is your cue to how long and involved your presentation should be. Are they giving you twenty minutes or two hours? Design your presentation to accomplish your goals within that time frame.

A few tips that you will want to keep in mind: Do everything you can to make the potential clients comfortable and make sure your presentation is complete, well-organized, and consistent. Your presentation should seem intelligent and assertive. It should demonstrate that your firm has talent and that your firm is a winner. Explain that this project is of interest to you, and exactly how you and your staff will be involved in this process.

Know your audience; research every possible part of the firm, both corporate and personnel. Do the same for a private client. The more history you have on the client, the easier it is to relate to them. It has helped me immensely to know what part of the country they came from, their education, social background, and religious and political affiliations.

The presentation requires first that you define your firm, its abilities, and your position with the firm. Second, you need to relate these definitions to the client's needs in a way that shows you understand them. The next issue is to define the quality of the project. What is their timetable? Involve the client. Restate their expectations and explain your own. Compare their existing project to similar ones from your files. Cover the issue of the budget. Explain the management processes common to this type of project, who will work on the project, and what their roles are.

When you write a presentation, select the primary point and build on it. Collect all the appropriate information and review, summarize, and simplify. Weave it together in a way that is easy for clients to absorb and process. Create a logical

Personal profile/special life events list:

sports
hobbies
work style
past work experiences
who really makes the decisions
what turns them on
what they dislike
real financial situation
attitude and method of using money
who their friends are
what their competition does and what it is
standards of the field

order. Listen to the client's pace to establish the timing or tempo.

If you are talking about new technology, be very, very careful to keep it simple. Relate that technology specifically to their situation, and don't give them too much technical information at this point. Don't just tell a client that a low-voltage lighting system is the solution; explain the workings of the system to the client and how it would be used on an actual job site. Letting a client see real-life application of a product allows him or her to become comfortable with the technology. Support your information with written or other materials that can be reviewed later, but don't leave more information than can be easily absorbed by someone outside the design field.

Give references. The prospect wants to know who you've worked for before on projects similar to their own. The next thing they want to know is how your firm differs from other firms. Keep any important facts on the first page of the agenda and make it very easy to read. You may be giving them a very thick presentation, but take into account that they are going to read the front page and the last; the rest of it they probably will never look at.

Make enough copies of the agenda for each attending member of the client's firm. This prevents their having to write down each detail and keeps their attention focussed on the presenter. The agenda should either be bound or presented in a formal, attractive manner with your company's name prominently displayed. Usually, clients see many people during a bidding period; you don't want them to confuse your firm with another.

You may want to include additional information on your group, such as magazine or newspaper articles or brochures.

Once you have your outline and agenda of what must be covered, take an appraising look at your visual aids. They should be designed so that they can be read twenty feet away. Do you want a slide show? A video? Don't frustrate or embarrass people by giving them something that they cannot read. This doesn't build a good rapport.

Make sure that you can be heard. If necessary, take a lesson or two in voice projection so that you understand exactly how you are speaking and how you are using your voice. Occasionally, you will find yourself making a presentation to an audience of older people. They're not extremely old, but they are old enough to possibly have hearing deficiencies. Make sure that they hear you. Speak clearly.

Dress in a businesslike manner. This tells the prospect that you consider this an important meeting and that you have come to them dressed with respect.

Rehearse your presentation on tape. Listen to it and play it again, repeatedly. Rehearse it in front of your staff and strangers; the more you do it, the better your presentation will be. I still rehearse all my presentations five to twelve times. I have learned that people who write well don't write a paragraph just once—they do it over and over and think nothing of it, just as we go back over our designs to be sure that they are just what they should be. A formal presentation needs rehearsal and review. If you're going to be good at it, invest time and effort in it.

Know your presentation. Have an outline if you need it. Reading from a script is unacceptable unless there is a question on a very technical issue and you want to refer to printed material to add authority to the answer. This should only be present on request; keep it simple unless the client also has indepth knowledge of the issue.

Always give your prospects something so that they leave with a positive feeling. It doesn't matter whether you give them a special idea or just put in a little extra effort on the presentation.

Consider the cost of the presentation. Your competitors may spend a great deal of money on presentation. Architectural firms customarily go to great expense to do perfect presentations. Consider these costs carefully. After all, you don't want to appear extravagant. You do want to appear as if you are professional, that you do care, and that you are willing to put the effort into the project. Generally, interior designers will spend about four to ten percent of their fees to get a job. This includes money spent on general promotion and direct marketing expenses for special projects. Established firms customarily spend four percent of their fees. However, a new firm may spend anywhere from ten to twenty percent. The newer the firm is, the more it costs to win projects.

Negotiating is another part of every presentation. Who is the best person to do this? It is usually best to share this responsibility within your firm, and for different people to work together. This is one reason that designers work in teams with other design professionals: they realize the strength in group practices, especially in negotiation. Should a difficult situation arise that you know requires negotiation, let the sales-person stay the good guy. Don't let him or her deal with the problems of a client he or she is attempting to sell. Appoint someone else to do it.

If you need to negotiate a very serious situation—something that is critical—recognize that the chief executive officer is probably the last person who should do the negotiating. Let me explain why. If I'm negotiating for you and I tell a client that I think the designer will accept certain terms, I still have the privilege of going back to you for approval. I can then return and renegotiate if necessary. When you are the designer on the spot and the final decision is yours, you don't have the option of renegotiating. So be careful in choosing a person to negotiate a particular procedure.

Finally, look at your presentation from the client's viewpoint. Are you giving them something that they really need, and do they believe in that need? If they believe in the need and see the value, then the relationship is developing well. Keep working at your dealings with your clients to establish that kind of a value relationship.

PUBLIC SPEAKING TO DEVELOP BUSINESS

Public speaking and presenting a project to prospective clients are somewhat similar in their requirements. The audience in public speaking generally is more diverse. Public speaking is included in this section because doing it well is a personal skill. If you are considering giving a speech, here are a few guidelines.

Speaking on the right subject has a strong marketing value. Make sure you know why you are there and what you want to accomplish, what the audience or organization wants from you and, in turn, how it will affect your future business. Otherwise, don't do it. Preparing a speech takes a great deal of time and preparation. Speaking can be a good marketing opportunity, but only if you are a well-trained presenter. Many professionals do well in presenting to individual clients, but are not trained to project to a large group. Even if you excel at presentations, don't accept an invitation to speak if the topic is not your specialty or if you are not well-versed on the subject.

Think about the information you're giving. When you start as a public speaker or write articles that appear in the trade magazines, you are educating your competition. All of your competition will know exactly what you have done, rest assured. Educating your competition does not enhance your firm's profitability. Is it something you want everyone to know about—or are you giving away trade secrets?

Research the subject; don't depend on just your own knowledge. Check with other sources to refresh your memory and pin down your examples. A good presenter will spend one hundred to three hundred hours of research for every forty-five minutes behind the lectern. Even if you know the subject thoroughly, a minimum of ten to twelve hours of preparation is needed, and a shorter speech takes even longer. People who attend lectures are often quite knowledgeable on the subject, sometimes more so than the design professional because they have spent their lifetimes studying it as a hobby.

Know your audience. Check carefully into their backgrounds. You want them to understand your material, so talk to them, check and be sure to use a familiar vocabularly, one that they will understand. The time they spend with you is valuable and expensive to them. They want to go home feeling they had a worthwhile experience. How many people will hear the speech or receive the message? Will presenting this information promote a relationship between you and your potential client? Or does it underscore your expertise in an area the client doesn't need? Is there anything in the speech or article that could jeopardize your business in the future?

Make sure you include some way for the reader or audience to reach you. Try to make sure the topics appeal to your potential clients. Consider both subject and potential audience as you decide whether it is really worth your efforts.

Appearance is important. Dress in comfortable clothing, but a little better, a little more formally, than your audience. Think about your posture and gestures. Over 75 percent of your impact depends on the way you present your material. Only 25 percent depends on the material itself. Comfortable shoes and clothing that doesn't restrict your movements are a necessity. You can tell when a speaker is not comfortable.

How do you sound? Professional training teaches people to use their voices as instruments in the same way as singers and musicians are trained. Pronunciation, enunciation, breathing, and timing affect the presentation. Monotone voices put an audience to sleep.

What are your speech habits? Overuse of "ums," "uhs," and "you knows" can dilute the effect of your presentation. A coach can help point these out and suggest substitutes. Pausing, keeping silent is better than "uh."

Tape yourself during the course of a normal work day or tape a presentation to a client. Then listen critically.

Check your equipment. There is a wide variety of audio-visual equipment today. Learn how to use it and which pieces are best for you. Arrive at least 1 1/2 to 2 hours before the program to make sure everything is in position, and that the equipment you need is there and working properly. Checking the room the day before is even better. Many speakers prefer to carry their own equipment so that they have control. It's really unfortunate if you start speaking and then find the equipment is not working.

Practice, practice, practice. This is the most valuable tip to improving your communication level as well as your comfort level. Tape each of your rehearsals. Perform in front of your friends and anyone you can trust to criticize your performance. Each time you listen to a taped rehearsal, you will find areas that can be improved. On your way to the presentation, play the tape again so that all points are fresh in your mind.

Professionals do what they are good at. If there is an area in which you lack polish, get a tutor. Take the time to do things well, or find someone who will do it well. Don't degrade your professional standing in a community by doing a poor job.

Chapter 20

Qualifying the Client

The first meeting with the client usually has a time limit, and you may only have one or two opportunities to convince the prospect that your firm is right for his or her project.

No matter how often you've done it, you still need to think about format. What information do you need before you walk into that meeting, and what should you leave with the prospect? Without an outline, you may miss some issues, and this can lead to later misunderstandings with the client.

Learn as much as you can about a prospective client. You need to know in detail exactly what they want, how they purchase design services, and what they know about interior design. Have they used designers before? Who did they use? What architect have they worked or are they working with now? What about other consultants? Who does the buying or the approving? What types of people are they? Can you communicate with them? Are these reasonable people? The way you dress is important; we need to dress according to the type of client and project.

Advance effort pays off a hundred-fold later. Taking the time to run a credit report protects you from becoming involved in a bad situation later on. Outlining or listing what you want to cover during your meeting will help you feel at ease, and you'll come out of that interview with the information you need. It's all too easy to become involved in great yet not totally relevant conversations. However, if you are not specific in your objectives, you run the risk of failing to obtain the information needed to develop the project.

A standard form will help with this process. One that works for my firm is included for you to look over and adapt to your individual needs. A very simple prospective Client Report tells you who you are going to see, where, and the directions on how to get there. It can be very uncomfortable riding around looking for a building, knowing that the client is waiting for you. Include the client's phone number so that if you lose your way or find you must be late, you can warn the prospect. Respect the client by being on time. Time is irrelevant to some people, but most people feel better about working with you if you are careful to be punctual. The client is evaluating you at the same time you evaluate them. Being on time is one way you enhance their perception of you as a professional.

The Prospective Client Report lists the type of project and the objective of the appointment. After the meeting, write on the form the outcome of the meeting and what preparation is needed for the next meeting.

At the bottom of the page is space for the date of the next contact, and for an indication of their financial arrangements.

We use the Prospective Client Report in determining whether to develop the client, and when. Are they to the point where we are ready to send a proposal, or do we need another interview meeting or two? If the project is one you would like to develop or if it is a sophisticated one, try to win the opportunity for additional time with the client or for touring the building. (There are many small projects at low budgets for which this is not practical.) The development process is part of your research. Often we acquire information that assists us in evaluating the project, so that our proposal can be on target. The client can see we have a special interest in their firm.

Very rarely is a proposal sent after the first meeting, because I use a Design Service Questionnaire to define the project, and it takes forty-five minutes to an hour to review this with the client.

How many interviews does it take to develop a project to the point where you can present a proposal and get it signed? This varies, depending upon the size of the project. If you're discussing small projects, yes, you need to work out some sort of proposal so that you can make this decision within the first interview. Larger projects may take weeks, many months, or maybe even a year or more. This is normal for large projects, and if you want projects on that scale, you will have to put in the effort.

RESEARCH

The more time you spend up front listening to what clients want and defining their needs and their projects, the less time you must spend later in designing the project and handling complaints at the end.

Research is the foundation of good client relations. Don't walk in to a new project without first calling around to try to learn how prospective clients have worked with other design professionals. Speak with other tenants in the building and neighborhood about what has happened on the site. Talk to anyone who knows the client and also knows your firm. The more information you have, the easier it is to communicate properly.

Run credit reports, not just to find out the firm's credit standing, but also to find out the personal histories of the people you will be working with and designing for. Who are the company officers? Are they management people, accountants engineers, or physicians? What are their professional backgrounds and lifestyles? Do anything you can to anticipate likely attitudes about the project. You want to know what this prospect knows about the design discipline, as well as the styles and methods they use to manage their company.

When you question the prospect, try to relate all design issues to items they have and can see in their individual spaces. This is why a personal visit to the site is so important: it's an opportunity to meet other people involved, whether it is family or staff. You may want to compare their offices to one of their competitors' offices, then to a similar office elsewhere in town. Although the other office may be attractive, perhaps you heard that it wasn't quite as productive. Did it meet their expectations?

What does the prospect think of the style of his competitors' offices? What firms does the prospect compare to his own? What do they expect of their clients?

Obviously, this type of information can be extremely important in planning the design direction for the new office they were considering.

You may be surprised by the amount of time clients spend on research. While talking to a client about carpet (there was a particular specification that I didn't agree with, and still don't agree with totally) I learned that three people on their staff had spent a year researching carpet backings. They had tested over thirty different samples on the floors of their facility and had worked with chemical research laboratories. I felt at that point that I should not even mention the other issues. It was best to use their work as a base and incorporate my design input.

WHO MAKES THE DECISIONS?

Very often a client doesn't realize or doesn't want to admit to you that he or she is poor at making decisions. That's why they hire you. When you meet a client, find out how they make decisions. Do they make it themselves? Is it a case where they must talk to their wives or other members of the board? Sometimes a man will not make any decision unless he has reviewed it with his wife because he feels that she has great taste.

It is important for the clients to see you as the qualified, concerned consultant. It is your job to narrow down the field of choices. It is important for you to place the client in a position where he can easily make the decisions. If this has not been done properly, obviously he is going to have difficulty.

Spend some time with your clients and prospective clients, and find out what their decision making processes are. Try to discover what you can do to make their decision-making process an easier one.

USING THE DESIGN SERVICE OUTLINE

Any time you work on a new project, it is important to be clear about exactly what the client wants and expects in terms of service. Most clients today do want, or need, a price. They're not happy to work on strictly open-ended contracts. To give them a price that won't be a source of trouble later, we need to define specifically what they want done. Start defining the project at the initial interview, using an outline of questions to make sure you cover all the issues. This is best done at a planned meeting, where the client knows in advance that it will take a span of forty-five minutes or more and has made that time commitment.

The Design Service Outline is written as a form, so that all you have to do is to write in, using a pencil, the client's responses. These may change during the interview. The Design Service Outline has two functions. Not only does it define what the client expects, it educates the client about the range of design services available.

Many interior design clients believe that we only select colors or develop space plans. Simply reviewing with them the general needs and the services on the Design Service Outline uncovers the extent of services available from the design field. We're not coming in and bragging to the clients about past work and our abilities. We're using questions that demonstrate our knowledge and allow the client to be the expert on his own space.

Although I fill in the form in pencil, it becomes part of the client's permanent file. Any designer, any person on the staff who works on the project can refer to this to see exactly what our responsibilities are and what someone else is taking care of.

The first page has a space at the top for the client's name and address, the name of the contact person, and the phone number. Who is responsible? Who contacted you? With whom will we be working and what are their phone numbers? On a residential job, it may be the husband, the wife, or another person who takes responsibility for the project. For a contract project, the contact person may be a facility manager, a vice president, or some other senior management person.

The next space is for the project as they define it, and this may change before the process is completed or even during the interview.

Who makes the decisions? This can vary considerably. It may be a participatory design process where the client wants to be involved in every small decision. Or it may be a corporate project where they really only want to hear about the major details with a complete overview and a total presentation.

Does the client want floor plans, boards, renderings, models, and do we believe the project warrants them? In what form are we presenting this job?

Who will we be working with? Who do they want us to talk to? Are there any other people they believe we should talk with? Are there others who, in their opinion, do not have the appropriate information? Maybe they don't want certain staff members exposed to the many details of this project. What staff are we to be involved with?

What other consultants do they have on board? Is the architect already involved? Is the engineer involved? Is there an acoustical specialist? What other specialists and consultants are already part of the project? Do others need to be brought in?

Have the contractors been predetermined? In some projects, the contractors are established and in place long before the design process is firm. In other cases, they are selected later.

At the bottom of the very first page is a space for the scheduled contact time, the time when you give the client his or her weekly update.

Page two of the form determines the functional and organizational requirements. Whether this is a residential or a contract project, there's always a space analysis, traffic flow, and a work flow. Are you doing the space analysis? Are you going to determine whether there will be any architectural changes or whether these spaces are appropriate for the functions for which they are intended?

Are you doing the traffic flow? Just how does this company function? Are we going to be responsible for directing the work flow?

What about the personnel? How many people work in this department? What is the expected growth?

What about the individual space requirement for each particular person? Sometimes this is determined by equipment use. In some large corporations this is predetermined by status. What is the company's standards and requirements?

What about visitors? Will they be permitted in all parts of the building or just on certain floors? What is the flow? What areas do you want to expose them to and which areas must be considered private? How are you handling these guests?

Every project involves equipment today, from the most technical commercial project down to the simplest of residential work. What type of equipment must be accommodated in this space?

The next issue is storage. What type of storage does the client need and where is it needed? Storage for record-keeping and supplies are part of almost every project. What other kinds of storage are important to this project and what must you supply?

Is the lighting to remain as it is presently, or is there an opportunity for lighting design? If so, who will be responsible for this?

What about acoustics? Every one of our projects has some acoustical detailing to it, because acoustics is a matter of hearing what you want and need to hear, and diminishing what you don't want to hear.

Audio-visual equipment seems common today. Who is responsible for the audio-visual planning for the space?

Security is one area where we ask that the client make a direct contract with the consultant or that the client specifically tell us that we are not responsible for security. This has become such a technical specialty today, and one that involves so much liability, that every design firm should be concerned.

What about the access for the handicapped? The Americans with Disabilities Act requires new buildings to meet certain federal and state accessibility standards. What does the client need? A residential client may be wheelchair-bound; may have accident-prone children; or may simply like the idea that people with even temporary physical impairments could move easily in the space. What do they see as their need?

The next page is blank. Because as you are talking, there are always unplanned details that must be noted, and this outline is structured so that you write down all the information you need to establish the requirements of the project. You may learn necessary details—ones that don't immediately seem to fit any category—in the course of conversation.

The fourth page is devoted to scheduling. What is the owner's projected goal for completing the project? For instance, they may expect to have the project completed in thirty days while you look at it as a three-year project. You had better determine this right now so that you can make changes, either in the scope of the project or in the completion date. Estimate the design schedule, work schedule, and the other issues.

Below the spaces for schedules is an area for notes where you can document preferences or details regarding the scheduling.

Page five covers the design concept. Will there be any architectural changes? If so, who—architect, engineer or other—is responsible for the changes? If not, does the building stay exactly as it is; are you merely dealing with the interior spaces, furnishings, and other interior details? Document all changes, details and finishes.

Under design concepts, you will see the floor plans listed again: the wall elevations, special details, cabinetry, or built-ins. Will you be designing those details, and are they included in your pricing? If you neglect to allow for this in your estimated budget, then you are responsible for providing all the drawings and the working details. This can really eat up your profit on the job.

What about the furniture? Are you using existing furniture, or does the client plan to purchase new furniture?

Has special equipment been assigned? Today there are few spaces, commercial or residential, that don't have televisions, computers, audiovisual equipment or other electronic devices. Each has special needs and requirements.

Whether there are window treatments, lighting, acoustical, security, and audio-visual, mark which areas you are responsible for.

The sixth page is devoted to project documentation. Floor plans: are you responsible for certain rooms or are all the rooms involved? The outline covers the furniture plan, the lighting plans, elevations, finish schedules (and any special notes you may need), hardware schedule, window treatments, and special conditions.

What about specifications? Will you be writing the bidding documents? Are you responsible for all the detail specifications? How much detail is enough for a pre-selected vendor? How much will have to be bid? The documents for one are considerably different from the other. Who handles the purchasing and what is your responsibility?

What about a maintenance manual? Obviously, these items need to be maintained. Who will be responsible for directing how this is to happen?

Is there a move involved? In most cases, whether it's remodeling or a new facility, some type of moving plan is required. Are you developing the moving plan?

The next page is dedicated to project management. Who coordinates the project? Is it the architect, another of the other consultants, or a contractor? Is the client the coordinator? Who is responsible for the overall coordination?

Who is responsible for scheduling, the shop drawing approval, supervision, and revision? How are they going to be handled? Does the client want you to include this in your regular price, up to a certain dollar figure, or is this to be billed as an extra and on what basis? Determining this right now can save trouble later on.

How will change orders be handled? Who will do the negotiating, prepare the pre-bid quotations, and handle the vendors and contractors?

What about payment authorization? Are you to approve items before they are paid for, or is someone else taking care of this?

Finally, will you conduct an occupancy evaluation, post-occupancy review, and others? The back page is left empty for your review.

Along with the Design Service Outline, we use an overview page for costing. We put each area from the outline on our cost-calculating sheet.

Suppose you are responsible for suggesting architectural changes that might be worked into the project. You are responsible for writing the specifications for all the finishes that are required and for preparing the furniture plan. A presentation from the acoustical engineer will be considered, but a separate quotation will be submitted, and on down the line.

The Design Service Outline is your master sheet for determining how to bill the project: whether it will be done on an hourly basis, with an estimated amount of time; whether it will be done on an over-contract basis; or by some other method.

You may want to calculate this in several ways. For example, after filling in the Design Service Outline, you can list every service and detail that the client requires. Then you estimate the amount of hours you expect it will take.

You also consider the length of time that the project will take to develop and complete. Scheduling affects your pricing. Is it a fast-track job or a very longterm job, and how much interaction will the project require? Will you need to send documentation to seven different consultants, or will you supply it to one person who takes care of everything? All of this is general expense and needs to be determined.

Once you have completed this sheet and you've worked out the estimated cost according to hours, then you may want to compare some other methods of evaluating costs, such as by square footage. Or you may even want to consider general estimated costs to complete a project, based on several other projects that you have in your file.

We find that this intensive background is absolutely necessary to give a client an appropriate method of working and an appropriate price. By the time you have finished going through the outline with a client, they understand a lot more about the responsibility of the designer on their project, and they can more easily figure out exactly what they want you to do.

It also protects you. Should you find, as the project develops, that the client is enlarging the project, you can refer them to your original proposal. "You will notice that in our initial proposal we did not include the fourth floor. We were only doing the third floor. If you would like us to handle this additional area, then we will send you a proposal to cover those areas." Or you may have it in your contract that you will agree to do these areas at an hourly rate, or an additional per square foot price. This can then be calculated and handled accordingly.

If we as designers are to run projects professionally, we need to start with a professional base. I don't see any way of doing it other than by using our experience and records, and evaluating what the client expects and wants from us. By balancing the two we should be able to come up with a system of working professionally because this is what clients need from us. They need that organization and they need that system.

This Design Service Outline is tailored for the needs of a specific firm and it has changed many times throughout the years. You will undoubtedly find that you need items that are not listed, but I offer my form as a guide to creating your own. We do ours in a very inexpensive photocopied form. We don't need anything fancy or ornate, just a form complete enough to include the details that you need on a given project.

This form stays with the project the whole way through. Our estimating sheet for the financial arrangements is on a separate page because that stays within the business office. There may be people working as consultants on the design project who need access to the Design Service Outline, but they should not have access to all the financial details.

Try using a Design Service Outline. I think you'll find it worth your while.

WHEN TO REFUSE A PROJECT

Undertaking the wrong project can hurt your firm, but how do you say no to the wrong job? One of the reasons you go out to see projects is to decide whether they fit your practice. The reality is that some projects don't fit. They're either much too large or too small. Remember the 70/30 ratio. If 70% of it is easy to do and you've done it so many times that you can do it almost with your eyes closed, then this is the job for you.

The challenging part should be no more than 30 percent of the project. If you need to learn more than 30 percent of the project, it's probably too risky for you to take it on. If more than 30 percent of the project is new, it will be difficult to make it unusual and creative. It takes too much learning time and extra effort, and it will be hard to get paid for it.

If during the interview or after your preliminary research you get an uncomfortable feeling, the best thing to do is to find a way to drop out of the project as soon as possible. The same applies when the job is not appropriate for your practice, or the client is not the type with whom you can work easily. Handle it professionally.

You might say, "This project is not our specialty. To do quality work for our clients, we find it best to stay with the type of work we're most familiar with." Suggest that when they have work in your specialty, they call you. You may even want to recommend two or three other designers they might contact. In fact, if you recommend other designers, it's always best to give them more than one person; it lowers your liability on the situation.

Or you might say, "Unfortunately, our schedule does not allow us to take on another project at this time." The client may decide to wait for you. If this happens, it also gives you time to do more research and see if the client's increased commitment may be worth your consideration.

But handle it with care. Sometimes your intuitions can be very valid.

HOW DO YOU FIRE A CLIENT?

No matter how careful you are, you may still have a problem client. Sometimes you think they're great at the beginning. But as soon as it becomes a problem, fire the client as quickly as possible. Tell him or her that the project is developing into something that isn't really working for you, and suggest he or she find someone else.

Suppose you are in the early stages of client development with a prospect, just past the Prospective Client Report and perhaps past the Design Service Outline, but not as far as the contract or letter of agreement—and you decide you don't want the client? Not too long ago, our firm heard that a prospective client was very litigious and had instigated lawsuits against several contractors. I was afraid that we were going to be the next to be sued, so I told the client that I was sorry, that we wouldn't be able to handle her project for her.

Unfortunately, as it turns out, the interior designer who took the job was sued and had a very difficult time with the client. She was not paid for her work, incurred heavy legal fees, and lost the major part of two years of her life.

If you are at all concerned about whether this client is right for you, perhaps that client *isn't* right for you. A designer who attended one of my seminars told the group that her partner refused to work for attorneys, and asked for our opinion. I asked why she felt this way. The answer was that her partner felt attorneys were impossible. Every time she worked with them, she was sued.

After hearing this, I thought her partner was wise; she was aware that she doesn't work well with attorneys. If she had trouble with them on previous occasions, it's probable she would have difficulty with them on future occasions. She does well with physicians, so perhaps she should stick to working with physicians. The fact that she has found her focus may be one of the most important things that has happened in her career development.

Prospective Client Report

Client: _____ Contact Person: _____

Referred By: _____ Position: _____

Address: _____ Phone Number: _____

_____

New Address: _____ Directions: _____
(if moving) _____ _____

Project:

Objective:

Needs:

Result of Meeting:

Research of Information Needed for Next Meeting:

Date of Next Contact:

Financial Arrangements:

© *Design Business Monthly*

Figure 20-1

Design Service Outline

Name: _____ Date: _____

Address: _____ Contact Person: _____

_____ Position: _____

Phone No.: _____

Project:

Decision-making Process:

Presentation Form: Floorplans:
                    Boards:
                    Renderings:
                    Models:

Stages of Decisions:

Client's Representatives:

Staff involved:

Consultants:

Contractors:

Scheduled Contact Time:

Design Service Outline

Figure 20-2a

Determining Requirements: (functional and organizational)

Space Analysis:

Traffic Flow:

Work Flow:

Personnel - Expected Growth:

Individual Space:

Visitors:

       Flow:

Equipment:

Storage: Records:

          Supplies:

          Other:

Lighting:

Acoustical:

Audiovisual:

Security:

Handicapped:

Design Service Outline

Figure 20-2b

Scheduling:

Owner's Projected Goals:

Design Schedule:

Work Schedule:

Other Issues:

Notes:

Design Service Outline

Figure 20-2c

Design Concept:

Architectural: Changes:

                    Details:

                    Finishes:

Floor Plans:

Wall Elevations:

Special Details:

Cabinet/Built-in Work:

Furniture:

Special Equipment:

Window Treatments:

Lighting:

Acoustical:

Security:

Audiovisual:

                    Design Service Outline

Figure 20-2d

Project Documentation:

Floor Plans: (areas or rooms involved)

Furniture Plans:

Lighting Plan:

Elevations: (areas or rooms involved)

Finish Schedule: (special notes to be included)

Hardware Schedule:

Window Treatments:

Special Conditions:

Specification:

Bidding:

Purchase Orders:

Maintenance Manual: (companies or products involved)

Moving Plan:

Schedule:

© *Design Business Monthly*　　　　　　　　　　　　　　　　*Design Service Outline*

Figure 20-2e

Design Concept:

Coordination: Client:

Consultants:

Contractors:

Scheduling:

Shop Drawing Approval:

Supervision:

Revisions:

Change Orders:

Negotiations: Prebid Quotes:

Contractors:

Payment Authorization:

Occupancy Evaluation:

Post-occupancy Review:

Others:

Design Service Outline

Figure 20-2f

Chapter 21

Defining a Project

In design projects as in business, it's necessary to define the priorities of the job. What are the most important things that the *client* wants to accomplish on this job? The Design Service Outline is a form that gives an easy-to-follow list, which defines all the priorities and directions of the project. It is important to understand the limitations of that job. Let the client understand that yes, designers can accomplish almost anything, but that everything has a price. Is service X really worth investing in? If so, if affects the priorities of the project. If not, something else takes precedence.

Not only should you list the priorities of a project, but also review it with the client several times during the project so that they are aware what priorities you are dealing with. It is possible their priorities may change during the project. If you don't keep checking with them, you could be unaware of the change. Because developing projects takes time, sometimes clients see other advantages, other things that can be done within this given space—and consequently their priorities often do change.

So clarify priorities carefully. This list will also help

ensure that you are paid for what you do. You based your quote on the outline. If there are changes, revising the priority list with the client gives you an opportunity to revise your price quote.

HOW MUCH CHANGE IS COMFORTABLE TO A CLIENT?

When you meet a new client, one of the first judgments you must make is how much change is comfortable for him or her. If a client is to enjoy a space and accept a space, he or she must feel comfortable in it. Anything we do to a space, any improvement, is change. Change always produces insecurity and some emotional resistance. When you are working on a project and developing a space, don't change it to the point where the client won't be comfortable with it.

Too much change can make us ill, according to psychologists. A number of years ago *Reader's Digest* ran a chart that let people evaluate the stress in their lives caused by various changes. Each change—getting married, loss of a spouse, loss of a child, changing jobs, and the like—was assigned a stress value, and when the total of these stress values reached a cutoff level, psychologists could predict illness.

Similarly, too much change in interior spaces is a mistake. I discovered, after doing projects with several corporations, that a vice president is often in charge of the new building. If that vice president develops a building which is a few steps better than what they presently have—one which helps them to develop their company within the next two to three years, yet is not necessarily state-of-the-art or the very best in every way—this particular person will very often become the chief executive officer and will go on to lead the firm. But if that vice president creates a state-of-the-art building for the firm, one that will carry them through into the next century, this person is often not advanced to such a high position, but is simply left in some lower management position.

In the latter instance, the change was too shocking. There may have been other factors as well. The corporate budget for building may have been overspent, even though in the long run it may have been the best thing to do. The new building may have caused havoc or an uncomfortable feeling within the corporation, and this unease may have cost them momentum in other areas. So the vice president in charge of the state-of-the-art building almost has never been advanced, despite the great thing he or she may have done for the company.

Interior space is one of the tools of a corporation, just as it is a tool for a family. We have to design within the parameters of what will be effective for their given life and work style; therefore, one of the best things a designer can do is visit the prospective client's site. See how the client has been working or living and determine the level of design. This also assists greatly when it comes to budget. Clients often say to us, "I don't want to spend too much money." But how much *is* too much? It's very difficult to tell without visiting the site, where it is easy to judge whether very expensive art furniture or fine quality products, like those of Vladimir Kagan or Baker, or other quality manufacturers were used in the previous job. If the site is done in hand-me-downs or "old attic," we know that their idea of low budget is very different from the client who has been accustomed to buying quality items.

One of the things that I have learned in my practice is that it is best to work within the range of where the client is, to educate them slowly to the design process. If we rate our projects on a scale of one to ten—with one or two indicating poor quality and ten very fine quality—and we accept an existing space rated a two or a three the best thing to do is to make that project a three, a four, or maybe a five if we want to keep the client. Taking it too much beyond that can be really destructive to the relationship

It's not too shocking to bring a site that rates a seven or an eight to a nine or a ten. But it is better to take the two or the three, bring them up to a five and then a few years later develop them into a six or a seven, than to go directly from a two to a seven. In the interim, the client will have been educated by the experience of living in that space and will then want a better design. As you work on the design project, make the client familiar with the changes as they occur so that they start to feel comfortable with the new design. Then when they move into the space, they know where each item will be placed, why the items are there, and the purpose of the design. Part of this design orientation is an orientation for how to live in the space—not just selling the design.

When setting up a project, prepare a values worksheet (See Figure 15-3) for the products you recommend. List each design feature or product you selected for this project. There is a reason you selected each product, a reason that you believe this designer product answers the client's need. List the particular problem that you feel the product solves or the benefit you think it has. Conclude this sheet with all the support information and documentation that you may have. This information can come from experience from other installations, manufacturers' specification or information sheets, laboratory reports or articles on products from magazines or journals.

Today we need a lot of support materials, both to reinforce our professional position and to lessen the liability of the professional recommendation. Put together all this information so that when you go to a meeting, you have all the back-up support data right at hand.

Keep that value sheet handy. Ask each staff member to use it when they're interviewing sales reps regarding a product that you might want to place in a project. Keep those values in mind as you look at different products because the time will come when you need to pull them forward. If you have them well documented, you'll be ready and be able to cover everything.

Interior design is a very sophisticated science and art today. When you are given a prescription by a doctor, you want to know what the side effects are. The client wants to know everything about the product.

To present your design specialty as it deserves to be presented, we must constantly keep in mind this need vs. value statement. We solve problems. We try to give the clients the best products. Be prepared to show just why and how you made your choices.

WHAT IS QUALITY?

What a designer sees as quality may not be what our clients see. Quality is the presence of value *as the client sees it.* You can expend a lot of effort to polish a project and still discover that the client wanted something different. Talk with your client extensively, in a regular programmed interaction to develop an understanding of their value system.

Management consultant W. Edwards Deming said, "There is no such thing as 'getting it right'. There is always a better way." As designers, we tend to think our way is best. We may direct the project and make many decisions, but the client *owns the project and pays the bill.* So from the first interview through all communication, keep classifying and charting the client's values. This awareness is the foundation for good communication and client satisfaction.

WHAT SHOULD YOU DO IF A CLIENT WANTS TO DO IT LATER?

When you're working on a project, very often clients will say, "I'm sorry, but I can't do this now. I would like to do it later." A lot can happen between the time you are first contacted and the time you begin to place the orders. The reasons a client holds up a project can be a change in lifestyle, a change of staff, or that the project is simply more expensive than they expected. It could be economic change: their business has increased and they don't have time to deal with an installation, or business has decreased and they no longer have the money.

Sometimes, it may be appropriate to encourage the client to complete a project now, when it fits into your schedule and you have the workmen available to do it. In situations where the client is just not comfortable with doing the project now, for financial or other reasons, what should you do?

My feeling is that it is better to do a project later than to have no project at all. If they're not ready to do it today, keep in touch with them. Be understanding. Let them know that when they are ready, you'll be very happy to work with them. If you never call them, they probably think you've lost interest. If you occasionally check with them to see if they are still interested or if their needs have changed, it may turn into a sale. A late sale is far better than no sale at all.

CLOSING THE SALE

How do you close a sale?   Well, really, I hope we never close a sale. Our objective is to build relationships, long-term relationships. That's what pays best for any professional practice. We don't want to start and finish a project—we want to build that sale! So, as you look at projects, don't think, "How do I close the sale?" but, "How do I develop the sale?" As you develop it, think of how you plan your rooms or the way you build a building. You first put in a secure foundation and then make sure that everyone understands that it is secure before you go on to the next course of work. You should be doing the same thing when you build a sale or a project.

So don't talk about closing a sale, talk about building a relationship with a client and developing it into a project. Deal with it just as you would construct a job or a building. This will give you a great basis for ongoing work.

A sale occurs when a need is converted to a want.

One of the most difficult parts of selling is knowing when and how to close a sale. According to Zig Ziglar, a best-selling speaker on the art of selling, "If you can't close, you can't sell."

Prepare a list of leading questions, questions that cannot be answered with a yes or a no. This requires the client to give an extended answer.

You might say, "Now that we've examined your plans, what other questions do you need answered before you are prepared to make a decision on the project?"

Or you could say, "Taking into consideration your work schedule, when would you like us to start the project?"

Other good questions are:

- What are your scheduling plans so that we can alert our studio to reserve time for the appropriate people needed for this job?
- When will you need specifications?
- Shall we start working on the final designs for you?

If you don't get a positive response to these questions, go back over the preliminary part of your presentation, restating their decisions to make sure you understand their position. Attempt to reorient or redefine the project.

It is important to keep an itemized list of every point you discuss on a project, as well as the results you achieved. File this list for reference during future contacts. (See Meeting List, Figure 15-2.)

Sometimes designers lose a project because they oversell. The client is ready to buy, and the designer talks too much about features of the project he or she considers special—and these may be issues that are irrelevant to the client. Losing a sale can sometimes occur simply because the designer neglected to ask for the job.

It takes an average of seven to ten calls to develop a client, and some designers stop too soon. Each time you meet, you should try to establish a date for calling a client before you leave his or her home or office. Again, build this process on values. First their values, and then the complement of appropriate design and product to develop their values. This creates and endorses want and need.

DEBRIEFING

Understanding why you didn't get a job is one of the best ways to learn. If you've made a presentation on a project and you suspect or know that it was awarded to someone else, follow up. Call the client and find out who was selected and why your firm wasn't chosen. Before you call or speak with the prospective client, prepare a list of questions so that you can develop the conversation and learn from it. Let the client know that the call is standard procedure, that it helps you better evaluate your position in the field.

Ask how the decision was made and who was selected for the project. Then ask how your presentation compared to the others, and what the client thought of your presentation. Finally, ask whether your firm could be considered for any other project he or she has planned.

Talking with prospective clients who decided against using your firm creates good will. Tell them that you enjoyed the opportunity to meet with them and to get to know them, and add that you would like to work with them in the future should they ever have a problem or a different need. Encourage them to call you. Be sure they know the door is open. Your goal is to leave the client with a pleasant and positive impression of you and your firm. You are professionally disappointed but not angry that you didn't get the project. You do not want losing this project to stand in the way of your being considered for the next one. (Figure 15-5 is a debriefing guide.)

THE CLIENT'S DUTIES

Before beginning a project, it is advisable to list in writing what you would like the client to do. Some of these issues may be part of your contract. If you are using a simple letter of agreement, give the client an outline of what you expect from him or her. Example: the client will supply you with all the information you need to do the job. This means the client should tell what you need to know to understand how their company operates, or how the family lives, because not everyone performs the same functions or lives the same way within a space. In order for you to be able to do your work correctly, you must be aware of the fine details of their particular way of working or their lifestyle.

The designer must be able to have access to this information from other knowledgeable people within the organization. Who are the right people to interview? This may be information that the chief coordinator does not have. Who will understand the future direction of the company and has the ability to supply the correct, detailed information?

You must have open access to the space. At what hours can you get in, who is responsible for letting you in, and just what are your privileges or restrictions in this operation? When can contractors work? Precisely what is convenient and suitable to the client?

Schedule regular meeting times. The client must give you a time each week for regular communication. You need to know to whom you are to be responsible. Whether it be a residential or contract project, there must be one person who takes this position. This person will be the one receiving the weekly calls. This person will be the one within the organization who is responsible for coordinating all of the issues relating to the design. Is that person also responsible for making sure that the equipment requirements are accurate so that when furniture is made to fit, there is no chance there will be a change? Who handles those details? This is why, on the Design Service Outline, we review the decision-making process.

THE PROCESS FOR APPROVAL

You need to know who's going to *sign* the *documents,* who is going to be responsible for all of your contracts, purchase orders, change orders, or whatever documents are involved in the project.

The client should be open with you about their feelings. If the client has questions, they must let you know so that you don't continue working on a design that may be inappropriate. The client must make every effort to make you aware of any problems as they arise.

The client must understand the financial arrangements. It is advisable to review these in the very beginning so that the client has an opportunity to prepare for these issues. That way, when you send the bill, they will be prepared to see that you are paid at the appropriate time.

The style of the decision making process affects their time commitment. If it is to be a participatory process, then the client must understand that he or she will be required to spend a specified number of hours per week with you. Going over this in advance will often help the client determine just what type of design process is best for them.

It is necessary to review the system for purchasing and contracting, so that the client understands that if this project is going to be managed, if specifications are going to be bid and if it's going to be put out to the lowest bidder, there are certain risks involved. It's a good idea to go over the different types of processes of completing a job before beginning a job. That way the client understands what the process involves and, therefore, is better able to determine whether they want you to obtain several prices on it and select from those preferred vendors, whether they really want to put it on an open bid, or if they want you to arrange for a turn-key project.

The major point of this is that you must take the time to go over the client's obligations with him or her as you plan the project. Usually the client's questions cover many of your needs. If further explanation is needed, provide it. It is wonderful to say, "we can take care of everything" and, in some instances, this might be the right way, but in other cases we may be getting ourselves into a situation which is far too risky for a designer to handle.

Go over these issues and let the client understand what it will take to complete the job, and just which method is most appropriate for this particular client and this job.

Chapter 22

Customer Service

What hours should a designer work? What are appropriate working hours? In the current market, there is no such thing as regular business hours. Many clients are unavailable during the day. If you want their business, you may have to organize your schedule so that you are available when they can see you.

Of course, you can tell clients that it is most advantageous to meet at your studio during normal working hours; however, other designers are adjusting their hours during this intensely service-oriented period, so you must as well.

Check with your clients to determine what is really needed, and make yourself available at a mutually agreed on time. To attract new clients, you may discover that you need one or two late nights a week. Many designers find that clients are not comfortable spending their productive hours buying design. Some studios find the weekends are their best-paying times. One of my best and largest accounts could only see me early in the morning—at 6 a.m. So we were finished with our decisions by 7:30 or 8:00 a.m. when the staff began to arrive.

This gave us a block of uninterrupted time and was very valuable in getting good decisions. It was well worth it, although I needed to be sure I was up and ready. Everything was ready the day before. I was up at 4 a.m., reviewed meeting notes from 4:45 to 5:30, when I left for the meeting. I tried to be five minutes early. I did this every Tuesday morning for 8 1/2 years. As a result, I wake up early. Some of my city friends don't understand this.

Should you give your home phone number? Perhaps. There should be some way for clients to reach you in an emergency. On the whole, clients will not take advantage of you if you demonstrate your proactive style of working by calling regularly with information.

What if a client asks your firm for a service it does not provide? If a client asks for a service your firm does not provide try to find a firm, or several firms, that handle that sort of request. Clients hire designers to make their lives more convenient. Many designers have built their practices by coordinating services for other needs. New people in a community may not know where to find needed services unrelated to design, such as cleaning or markets. Help them if you can. It is better to have them depend on you rather than on someone else. Be careful who you do refer, but try to be helpful. It is usually appreciated.

What do we need to do to keep our clients? A present client is worth more than a new one. Keep in touch with your clients. Sport them; relate. It costs us at least five to seven times as much to nurture and develop a new client as it does to maintain an existing client. Existing clients know about you, have bought from you before, have worked with you. So nurture them, keep them and develop them.

What do your clients think? Nothing is more valuable than your reputation—the way your clients think of you. **And unless you ask, you may never learn what they really think.** After clients have lived in a project (job) for two years, our firm asks, "How did you find our services? How did our firm relate to your company? Were we easy to work with? What were the hard parts about it? What would you suggest that we change in our process?"

Sometimes the answers cover issues the firm hadn't even considered, but were very important to the client. Sometimes these issues will be important to other clients. Interview your clients, and see if their suggestions might help you in designing your program to better suit the next client.

Talk to clients often. Ask what your firm can do to make the project better. In their opinion, do you deliver on time what you promise to deliver? Do you do things right the first time or do you have to do it over? Other questions you might ask are:

> Do we listen to you?
> How hard do you think we're working to keep you happy?
> How much confidence do you have in our services and our products?
> How well do you think we understand you?
> How well do you think we understand your special needs and requests?
> How do you rate our design studio?
> How do you rate our staff and our service?
> Is the staff helpful and polite?
> Do we speak your language?

Before changing your firm's direction, ask your clients.
Before you consider any major changes to your customer service program, check with your clients and find out what they really want and then test some of your new ideas. Ask them whether they feel this is a better way. Try it out on some of your employees and on different people that are part of your company. After you find that it really works, put it into action. There is no point in making major policy changes before you are certain that these are what clients really want and need.

Design firms need to organize themselves so that they meet the needs and services of the client. Sometimes the services we offer are not what clients want. We need the skill and knowledge to be able to evaluate the client's needs and find ways of putting them in place. Interview your clients and learn how your firm measures up.

Keep your promises. Don't promise anything you can't deliver. If you tell a client a project will take six months to complete and you finish it in four, you are a hero. If you say it will take six months and it takes eight, as far as they're concerned, you're a louse.

If you promise to make a phone call at a certain time or to be in touch with them, do it then. Honor your telephone appointments in the same way as you would honor in-person appointments.

Plan for mistakes. When you set up a project schedule, you hope and expect everything will go according to plan. Twenty, thirty, forty, even fifty percent of the time, everything will occur as planned: but that doesn't always happen. So have a contingency plan for mistakes, delays, and bad luck. Make a list of what could go wrong and make sure you have standbys ready.

When part of a project must be assembled in front of the client, test it beforehand so you know that the pieces fit together and how they fit. Take the extra time to check on an item's condition before it is delivered.

Develop resources to obtain what the client wants. If you don't have what a client wants, do you have resources which can supply them? If you are a small design firm, you need to develop ways to fill in some of these gaps. I saw an interesting practice in the South, which I believe is worth emulating.

The designers worked very closely together; they interacted as friends. Each designer had a key to the other designers' studios and would take items they needed—lamps, accessories, other small items—and leave a note. There was a constant trading of products. It allowed them to offer their clients a more total project than they could have offered independently.

Working together does pay. Find someone you would like to work with and see if you can trade and share both products and staff. This works especially well for large installations. We will often borrow staff from another firm. They understand how to do things, and both staffs enjoy the experience of working together. We get to see things that other studios have done and techniques that we may not have tried, and they in turn can pick up tips from us.

Show appreciation. Show your appreciation, not just to your clients but to your staff. Demonstrate that they are part of the job and that you value their help in making this design project what it is. Do something occasionally for the staff or the people who are supplying you. Send them lunch, invite them to a special party, send them theater tickets—do something that lets them feel they are special. Then the next time someone asks them whom they recommend as designers—a question which contractors are often asked—perhaps they will mention your firm.

We all want some form of acknowledgement. By acknowledging clients and staff, we build a stronger business. We shouldn't just stop at acknowledging the clients, but also let employees, contractors, and consultants know they are important to your firm. If staff members feel important, they will work better and produce a better project for your clients. So be sure your staff feels good about themselves. Thank them for what they've done.

Train your clients to work with you. Train your clients to work with you to obtain the best possible service from your organization. Most of our clients do not understand the process of interior design. It is often necessary to prepare the client for the types of people and processes that their project involves. Clients need to know this to understand how to interact, as well as the kinds of information we need, appropriate time schedules, and when it is best to reach them.

You need to train a client to understand how often and what kind of interaction is really needed from them. Unless you tell them, they won't know what they can do to build a stronger relationship with your company. They won't know how to react to the various craftspeople, vendors, and other consultants who work on the project.

Sometimes it's best to tell a client, "To reach me, call in the morning between 7:30 and 8:00 a.m., or leave a message at the office. I'm usually able to return calls at around noon or 4:30. A great deal of my time is spent on job sites or in vendor factories and I want your file in front of me when we talk. Since there are so many details on your job I want to be sure all the issues we discuss are correct. When craftspeople are working in the space, it is advisable to keep everyone who is not directly involved in that aspect of the job away from them. Any kind of distraction can decrease the quality of the project. They are artists too and it's not good to interfere with their progress. For example, if carpet is to be installed, the space must be at a certain temperature, appropriately cleaned and prepared. The right work environment is critical to the quality of the job.

Chapter 23

How to Handle Complaints

When a client calls with a complaint, he or she is often quite emotional, even irate. You can turn a complaining client into a positive one, and perhaps an even better client than before.

Most complaints come in by telephone, and this can intensify the problem because you are not dealing with the client face to face. Attitude is important. The problem can escalate, or you can let the client know you really want to hear what they have to say.

I've learned to say, "Excuse me a moment. I want to get your file. May I call you back in a few minutes when I have all the details in front of me?"

Another approach is to thank them for calling you because you want to hear the whole story. You *need* to hear from them because they are the ones you are trying to please. Then let them explain.

During their explanation, ask for clarification on important points; ask them to review all the fine points. Then ask if there was anything that was done correctly. Is the project totally wrong or it is just a phase or two that needs correcting. Finally, ask for the client's recommendation on how to handle it.

Perhaps the client just can't understand why they are being billed for such an item. In our case, a client called to object to being billed for a particular fee. He was used to paying bills for furnishings and for our design contracts, but these were defined in a different way. It was an add-on project, and our contract had clearly stated our billing procedures, but perhaps he didn't look at it.

I asked him to explain the situation, and when he had finished giving me all the details, I asked him to let me explain our billing procedures. If we're not billing correctly, either by the correct word usage or by our presentation, it is important for the client to tell us. It is harmful to any company to have an area of communication that is not presented clearly. I thanked him for taking the time to call me and told him he had brought up a number of points I hadn't considered.

Our position was that in the case of this add-on contract, we had handled details involving other contractors. The problem contractor's quote had included his supervision but he had left the job. So in order for the project to be completed, we assumed some of those responsibilities. These emergencies are generally the ones that get us into trouble. You want to keep the job moving. You don't want workmen standing around doing nothing; you don't want to waste the client's money; you want the job finished by the deadline. So you do one of those *right* things without proper documentation or authorization. (This was before fax machines.) Actually our billing was well covered in writing, but the wording we had used was not what he was accustomed to.

We received no financial compensation for any of the contracts and were not paid in any other way for these efforts. It seemed most effective to bill the client on an hourly basis for time spent. We could have billed on a percentage basis, or as part of the contract, but, this, in our judgement, was the better way.

Then I asked the client to tell me where we had gone wrong. He replied that he thought it had been presented correctly, and that he just hadn't understood it. Then he thanked me for taking the time to explain it.

It wasn't the time that I spent explaining it to him, it was the time I spent listening to him carefully, making him define each point and writing it all down so I could give direct replies that resolved the situation. He also saw that I had a description, a reason, or an explanation for each issue, so he knew I had paid attention to him.

In almost any court situation, the reason the client is suing is not the actual issue of the suit; it's that they felt they weren't getting enough attention. They didn't feel important! They wanted more attention from the design firm. Good telephone manners can help this.

Any time a client calls with a complaint, ask for details. Ask if you can tape the conversation, and explain that you want the entire design group and the factory to hear it so they can better understand the nature of the problem. Then ask the client to detail each point.

It's amazing how the attitude changes. Immediately, the client becomes more specific and less emotional. Instead of an emotional, exaggerated explanation, you receive the particulars of the issue. Your request for details proves that you take their problem or complaint seriously. Not only should everyone on the team know about it, but you will also take action. By acknowledging the client's problem, you have acknowledged its importance. This is the best way to handle complaints.

Don't stop there. Make sure that complaint is taken care of promptly. Whatever it takes, see that it is done immediately.

Unfortunately, designers must often wait a long time for the resource companies to respond to the complaint. This means the designer must step into the gap and handle the problem itself, and then deal with the supplier. Every design firm should have a budget dedicated to handling complaints.

Often design firms are asked to handle problems that have nothing to do with the part of the job that we handled. It doesn't matter. If the client perceives the problem as your fault, *you* have to find a way to fix it because it is your credibility and reputation that are on the line.

Turn complaints into positive opportunities to build future sales by fixing the problem immediately. Maintain a budget to handle problems. If you have a great year and the problem fund is unused, divide it among your employees who worked hard that year to prevent complaints. This is a good way to reward excellence.

Chapter 24

Contracts and Letters of Agreement

Almost every designer can tell you a sad story about the time they didn't have a contract or forgot to get an issue in writing. Protect your relationship. Give your client the documents, and be sure they sign them. This ensures that the client has seen the contracts.

Major disagreements between a client and designer usually arise from a breakdown in communications and can unfortunately, lead to lawsuits. To avoid being sued, assume nothing, and document everything in contracts or letters of agreement. These should be written in legal terms, but as clearly as possible.

Will contracts and letters of agreement protect you? To a certain degree, yes. But there is probably no contract that can be written that someone else can't get out of. You use a contract or letter of agreement to state your way of working. They define and make the client aware of potential problems. They acquaint clients with trade terms and familiarize them with the ways that designers charge and calculate their fees.

Many designers prefer to use contract documents prepared by the American Society of Interior Designers (ASID). The AIA has prepared similar contracts for use by architects.

These have become a standard and are generally accepted by clients. Legal advisors who work with design firms suggest that this standard form stands a better chance of being upheld in court than documents specific to a practice or client.

The purpose of a contract or letter of agreement is to minimize your legal and financial exposure. Consider your situation. Some very large firms still use a one-page letter of agreement. Others use contracts containing seventeen or more pages. Be sure you understand the contract, or don't use it. If you are an interior designer and decide to develop your own documents, the ASID contract is your best source of information. Take the standard ASID contracts (as well as any standard documents you can borrow from other design firms) to your attorney and ask him or her to review the contract provisions, taking into account the types of jobs you do and the issues that have caused you problems in the past. Ask that attorney to prepare an appropriate letter of agreement or contract for you to use. Read it carefully and be sure you understand it before you send it out.

You need some form of a letter of agreement or a contract to cover every project on which you work, small or large. In fact, any billing for more than $500 must be in writing as a letter of agreement or contract. Otherwise, it's not collectible.

Some of the issues you should include are specific to your locale and type of practice. Some very large projects are done with simple letters of agreement. In more litigious areas, accepting even a small project without an extensive contract could be risky.

HOW TO USE A STANDARD CONTRACT

If you are an interior designer, always use an interior designer's contract (ASID). If you are an architect, use the AIA contract.

BEFORE PREPARING A CONTRACT OR LETTER OF AGREEMENT

Before you prepare a contract or letter of agreement, you should think about:

1. A definition of the scope of services: What services are to be rendered, and what is the extent of the designer's responsibility?
2. The schedule: What will happen when, and whether, any part is contingent on other parts of the process for which you are not responsible.
3. Who is involved: Have a list of the people who will be working on the project and what their responsibilities are.
4. Quality of job: efforts and time required to produce this quality of project.
5. Risk: Client history, firm experiences, and other considerations need to be reviewed. Some projects have very heavy risk—high liability.
6. Terms: What does the client expect from us? How are they to work with? What must we do to complete the job in an outstanding fashion in their eyes?
7. Price: What can be charged for this type of project at this time considering general business environment, value of project competition, client's method of working?

Legally, an interior designer does not have the right to use an architect's agreement; only a registered architect can do so.

Make sure you understand the contract. Don't ask anyone to sign anything you don't thoroughly understand yourself.

Be sure that this contract or letter of agreement applies to the project. Modify the standard language according to the project so that it specifies whether you are working on a medical center, law office, or a residence.

Design the contract, if possible, to maximize the economic benefits so that you don't restrict your firm so much that you can't give them a good job. It is usual to have changes during a project, so plan for them and specify how they will be paid for to avoid problems.

WHAT TO PUT IN A CONTRACT

Contracts and letters of agreement should define what services you will perform, state the schedule for performing them, and name the persons who will carry them out. These documents should give all the details also of the way you handle charges, billing, and collection.

1. Describe what design services you will perform, along with your responsibilities. Generally, when a contract document that is ambiguous or incomplete goes to court, the ruling is against the author of the document. So say what you will do, and then do it. Specify what the client is responsible for. Present yourself as someone who can take charge of a project, yet don't oversell. It's too easy to say, "Don't worry about it, we'll take care of it." Be careful what you commit to because it is not always possible. It is more prudent for a design firm to offer fewer services, just those it can perform securely, than to offer services that may put the firm in jeopardy.

2. State in detail the amount of payment you expect and how it will be computed. Describe the method of billing, whether it is hourly, daily, on a percentage or a specified total-project cost basis, and include a payment schedule. It is so much better to say that payments are due when certain phases of a project are completed. Then you can plan ahead.

3. Explain in detail all your billing and collection requirements. You need this for your paper trail. Ask for as much payment in advance as you can. How can you design the cash movement to put you in the best position? Is there a way to be paid more quickly? Define your policy for late payments. How can you outline this so that the client is responsible for any costs that might be incurred?

4. Put a stop work clause in your document. Legally, you cannot stop work without one, even if you are not being paid. You also will want to include a restart fee for any project that is stopped for thirty days or longer for any reason. That length of time away from a project means you will have to review the project to start it up.

5. Termination fees also need to be discussed. If, for any reason, the client decides to stop the project, what is your policy?

6. An automatic escalation cost allowing for an increase in fees after twelve months or a certain given period of time can prevent your being locked into working at a set fee while your costs escalate.

7. Limit your liability on the project, if at all possible. Your liability should be based on the net fee for the job. If your fee is $3000, you don't want to be responsible for $300,000 worth of merchandise that could have been destroyed in the process.

8. Be careful of the way your contract lists prices to be charged. You cannot control your suppliers' price increases.

9. Your stated schedule should take into account that there may be delays for items over which you have no control. If the project will take six months for design, ordering, and installation, it is safer to say your firm will finish the project three months after the completion of the construction. Also, don't allow your firm to be held accountable for atmospheric conditions. Some things simply cannot be done at certain temperatures, or in extremely wet or extremely dry weather.

10. Spell out the duties and obligations of each party involved in the project. If you need support documents and cannot continue beyond a certain point without them, make their delivery part of the contract. The absence of specifications or engineering and architectural documents could delay the project or add to your liabilities.

11. Note that your design detailing relies on the work of other people. If you are relying on information from a particular source, list it, whether it is architectural prints or client's specifications. If a problem arises from an error based on faulty information, this could give you a legal out.

12. Stipulate who owns the drawings and specifications. You may be liable for design or material failures if your client uses your documents for a different project that has different requirements. Copyright these documents. If your client needs to own your specifications, you should retain your ownership of the copyright. Retain the right to use your design and documents; you should be free to adapt the details to other projects, publish them, or use them any other way you see fit. Consider the possibility of licensing the documents. You may want to allow the client nonexclusive rights to copy and reproduce the documents for a specific project. Make sure this license is not transferrable to any other project. Don't stamp the drawings or have them stamped until they are paid for. Be careful to mark your drawings that the prints are for reference only, for use by the various vendors and the contractor.

13. Spell out exactly how changes will be handled. In the precontract phase, decide how additions or deletions will affect your fee or charges. Require clients to sign and date all drawings and changes so that this does not become an issue

at a later date. Often projects grow as the work starts. Tell the client in advance that additions affect the cost of the project, and how they are billed.

14. Disclaim responsibility for changes made by anyone but yourself. Small changes can influence the quality and safety of the design. With this disclaimer, the minute anyone else makes a change, you are relieved of responsibility for the total project.

15. The client liaison should be specifically named. You would like to know the person who is responsible for scheduling and for controlling the job.

16. If the project requires certificates for flame proofing, flame retardant or other such safety aspects, have the appropriate agencies send them directly to the client's project—so that way the agency is responsible, not your firm. Likewise, have any guarantees for the project sent directly to the client so that if problems should occur, the guarantor is responsible.

CONSIDERATIONS

Those are the basics. You also may want an agreement stating that if schedules are met and the budget adhered to, perhaps your firm will be hired for the next project.

Some firms include the client's permission to publicize the project as a standard part of their contracts and letters of agreement. This includes photographing the project.

Designers who get sued are often designers who are not giving their clients enough time. If you are really working with a client as a teammate on the project, then you won't have problems, or at least in most instances you won't have problems. Firms end up in court when the client feels neglected.

Look to reduce your liability wherever possible, but also remember that you must offer the client a good project or they won't hire you again. Therefore, you must take on certain professional responsibilities. I know that attorneys suggest that our letters of agreement and our contracts should be designed so that they protect us completely. I'm not sure that this is ever totally possible.

Accept jobs that are appropriate to your firm, projects where you can satisfy clients. Keep a close rapport with those clients. Keep in mind that you are building this practice first for client satisfaction. If they are satisfied, they're likely to hire you again and they will give you a good reference.

In instances where the client writes the contract for a project, as often happens in a large corporation, ask your attorney to review both your contract and the client's contract to be sure they are in harmony.

Where there are overlapping responsibilities, clarify how these will be handled. A contract that involves other architects or contractors should clarify which items are included in your fee. For example, a phrase in your contract could say that since you are involved with the selection and detailing of items involving lighting fixtures, wall coverings and paints, floor coverings and finishes, custom hardware, cabinetwork, other custom woodworking or doors, that these will be covered under the fee for interior design services and, although these items may be purchased by the contractor, the percentage-of-fee billing does apply to them.

Chapter 25

Charging for Your Services

Charging for your services is part of the business relationship you have with clients. You must do it well enough that you feel adequately compensated for your time and efforts, and still have the clients feel they are receiving value for money.

Determining the appropriate fee structure for a job is of primary importance for your firm's development and profitability. The standard set by the proposal either gives the firm an opportunity for quality design work and profit, or creates a losing situation. If the project is not priced and structured properly, everyone loses. The firm and the staff lose because working on a job that is not a winner is upsetting: the job loses them money, and it could also cost the firm future jobs. The client is the big loser, as he or she does not receive a first-rate design.

You will not produce the job you want if you see the firm is losing money. Plan for variables. If the client wants an exceptionally high-level job, this may require additional research and development time to determine just what is needed.

JOB PRICING
When pricing a job, there are four things to be considered:
1. Scope of the job;
2. Services to be rendered;
3. Staff required; their time and cost;
4. Schedule.

When we do things free of charge, clients see no value in what we do.

Pricing, designing, and managing interior design is different than in any other design discipline. Although we can learn from the examples of the other practices, we are not the same. Interior designers expect to spend time doing finely detailed work. Often architects or other design professionals take on interior design and detail it just as they would an architectural project. This can only work for a very architectural project.

Know the job thoroughly and develop it with care. There is no quick-sell today. Before you even think about estimating a project, define precisely what it entails, using a checklist similar to the Design Service Outline (see pages 252–255). A detailed project evaluation, documented at the precontract phase, can also help clients understand just what your design services encompass and the costs involved. They can see that additional items will require an additional contract or fees, depending upon the proposal.

Know the job plan so that you can structure it for a good quality design process. The Design Service Outline helps in defining the job, the services to be rendered, and the scheduling. You should process and complete this form, and then review it with the others who will be involved in the project. It is important to have the project manager, or a person responsible for programming the project, assist in preparing this outline and the costing-out of the project. This enables him or her to understand both the project and the project goals.

This effort to define a project will permit you to examine carefully the total project. You will then know how to quote on it and also whether it is an appropriate job for you.

THE ART OF THE ESTIMATE

Estimating well is difficult. The ability to draw up good proposals and estimates is an art, but good up-front review and coordination makes it achievable. Carefully defining and qualifying a project is the best way to determine the appropriate charging methods. Design firms usually invest large amounts of time on these efforts; a week or more is not unusual for a larger project. It is much better to invest a week's labor to be sure that the job is right for the firm and priced correctly, than it is to take the wrong job and risk losing six months of fees.

Learn as much as you can about the client's past experiences in buying design so that you can present your proposal with references he or she understands. Ask staff people to estimate the time they will need for their parts of the projects, and compare their estimates with past records of similar projects as a safeguard. Some staff members tend to underestimate, while others are more accurate. The person preparing the estimate will have to make adjustments accordingly.

Obviously, the time scheduled can affect the cost of the project. The way your proposal is written strongly dictates the management style for the project. If your proposal catalogs all the processes that are to be done, then your project management list is almost complete. You know exactly who is going to do what when, and approximately how long it will take. Without the project plan in place, it is almost impossible to make an appropriate estimate. As you write your estimates and your proposal, try to do so in a fashion that will make later programming easy.

At this time, there are no official sources for standard fee scales for design work. Magazines occasionally publish lists of what has been charged, but these lists are not always accurate or believable.

When estimating or creating a quotation, work out several different quotations and compare them. Use different methods to arrive at these figures; a square-foot price; a dollar volume price of the estimated furnishings and finishing costs, plus a percentage; and an hourly estimate of the professional time that will be needed to handle the project. Then use the method, or combination of methods, that is most suited.

Before beginning estimations on any project, you need to:

1. *Define the scope of the work.* What needs to be done? What position will you play? What kind of project is it? Are there any high-liability issues? Is the project one that will require a lot of research, or is it a job you can manage comfortably? How prepared is your firm for this project? If it is a bank project and you have just designed fourteen other banks, then certain procedures will go much faster within your firm. If you have not designed a bank for a year or more, the project will be a bit more difficult.

Check out a job. If it is your type of job, it is worth putting effort into the proposal and into the presentation. If it is not the type of job that is right for your firm, then do not waste your time writing a proposal.

2. *Determine the expected quality of the project.* Does it require high quality finishing details, or is it simpler? What kind of quality has the client received on other projects?

3. *Evaluate the design team.* The architect, the design professionals, the contractors, and other professionals that have been selected will affect you and your team.

4. *Consider the schedule.* Is it a fast-track job or is it one that will take several years to complete? Review your proposal with the design professionals who will work with you on the project, for feedback and time estimates. This personalizes their investment in the project, and they will feel greater responsibility to complete it within the period of time they specify.

5. *Investigate the regulations and codes that apply to the project.* Are there many city and state codes or corporate standards that must be met?

6. *Assess your competition.* How does your firm compare to other firms bidding for the job?

7. *Predict what you will gain from the project.* Can you make a profit on this project? How much risk is involved? Will the time commitments or other restrictions on this project jeopardize your firm's profit opportunities on other projects?

As you consider each job, look at it in terms of the benefits you can expect to accrue from it. Balance your financial expectations and the amount of time you expect to invest in the job. Also consider the marketing value of the job. We have all done jobs that were not overly profitable but which later brought us several jobs that were profitable.

Calculate what this job means to your studio. Every now and then it is worth taking a job without much profit if it offers other benefits. It may offer an introduction to a specialty, give you an opportunity to test the waters. When considering entering this type of situation, do so with your eyes open.

If you want to change your specialty, you may find that you need to gain some credentials within the field. This may mean taking a project at a lower fee or even without fee in order to gain background and experience within this specialty.

8. *Evaluate the client.* Is he or she accustomed to working with an interior designer? Has he or she had experience either with your firm or with other firms? What kind of decision maker is the client? How many meetings do you expect to have? How many alterations are going to be required? What kind of rapport do you have with the client? Are you going to get along easily or will it be difficult for you?

BASIC METHODS OF COMPENSATION

There are many ways of charging, and the interior design field varies considerably from the architectural field in the projects that are profitable. Normally, architectural projects have a higher dollar volume than interior design projects, although labor and detailing on interior design projects are far more extensive. In my experience, the most profitable projects are generally those that have a mixed method of charging.

Many interior designers charge a straight hourly rate. Others charge an additional percentage on each item purchased, or keep a percentage of the cost of the total purchases. Some discount the retail price; others add to it. There are so many equations for how to charge that it is almost impossible to give anyone a guideline without reviewing his or her own requirements and expenses.

Hourly rates fall within a wide range and vary considerably. Right now the field is more competitive than it has been, and some rates have even decreased. So while some interior designers charge $35 to $50 an hour, and others $75 to $125, still others claim to receive $350 to $500. At $500 per hour, I wonder how many hours they're actually selling.

Some firms believe that charging by the hour is the best and safest way to charge. It is safe because you charge for what you do, and if you can find a client that will not set a limit, this is great. On the other hand, I have never seen a firm acquire great wealth by charging by the hour, especially in today's market.

To figure out your cost per hour, look at your cost for employees, overhead, and other expenses. Ask your accountant to work out for you how many billable hours you have per week. Generally, if people are working a normal forty-hour week, they probably are billing about thirty to thirty-five hours. There are design studios that require their designers to bill forty hours a week. Either they're cheating or adjusting their time somewhat, or they're working a lot of overtime that doesn't go on their timecards. It's pretty hard to bill forty hours if you are working forty hours. In fact, it's almost impossible. Look at your situation. How many hours per week are you billing out of your studio? Can this be improved realistically?

Are you generating income from anything other than hourly rates? It's very difficult to run a studio and to cover all overhead costs strictly on an hourly rate, unless you have a very large studio. The most profitable studios in our country have fewer than five or more than fifty people. It is very difficult to run these mid-sized companies profitably. Because of the creativity they require a lot of coordination, which makes them expensive to manage.

When you are larger, the cost of these expensive people is minimal. In larger firms, it is normal for the top person, the CEO or the principal whose job is primarily marketing and managing, to have few or no billable hours. Certain studios structure themselves that way. They feel that it takes a certain number of people to generate the business to keep the others fully billable.

Review your structure and your staff to fit what is practical for your area. Even if you don't charge by the hour, keep close tabs on exactly how many hours you're putting

---

ESTABLISHING YOUR OVERHEAD COSTS

Today, overhead expenses can vary considerably. Have your accountant or business manager calculate your overhead number so that you can determine what multiplier is appropriate to cover your overhead. This usually does not include any direct expenses, which are also billed to the client. Direct expenses normally include blueprints; reproductions; illustrated drawings; models; all of your travel expenses; postage; and freight. Some firms charge a percentage for these direct expenses to minimize the bookkeeping.

Review all overhead costs, or fixed expenses, such as:
• rent
• taxes and licenses
• insurance
• utilities
• telephone
• advertising
• marketing
• office expense
• automobiles
• dues and subscriptions
• loan payments
• management personnel whose time is devoted to business development or management.
• nonbillable support staff

---

into a project. Then you will know what you should be charging and what profits are actually being generated by that type of job.

Time-based fee. These are structured in several different manners. This is a safe and basic way of charging. However, because the clients may be concerned about overall cost, there are often limits or restrictions put on it. If the client is accustomed to working with your firm, then an open-ended contract is okay.

To determine your multiplier, add DPE (Direct Personnel Expenses) (refer to the *Interior Design Business Handbook* for details).

Hourly rate + Benefits = DPE

Add in your overhead expenses (see box for details). Your accountant will help you in establishing a percentage that must be added to the DPE.

Third, add in your proposed profit.

Time is calculated at: DPE × Multiplier of usually 3 to 3.5 × DPE. Today some firms are working on as low as 2.5 to 2.7 percent.

Time and expenses, open-ended. This fee for a project based on time and expenses is among the safest and most profitable ways of quoting if you can negotiate it open-ended with no limits.

Time and expenses with upset limit. This is time and expenses with a "not to exceed" or a guaranteed maximum. This gives the client a comfortable advantage, but can be costly to a design firm. Only very experienced firms can be confident of making a profit when using this method of charging. If you use more time, it is your loss. If you use less time, then you are also not paid, so it is your loss again. This contract must be carefully written to demonstrate specifically what work is to be done.

Time and expenses, estimated amount. This is a safer method, charging for your time and expenses within an estimate based on a scheduled estimate of time. The advantage is that it is more flexible. If the job ends up being more complex than you had anticipated, there is at least a range or a structure for covering some extra charges.

The way you charge can limit or increase your profits. If your rates cover only time and expenses, and you are paid by the hour, you have not risked much because you know that your profit is built into your multiplier and that you will be reimbursed for all expenses. This is an up-front agreement. While it is safe, it offers no change for a great profit. Unless you have your multiplier and your firm structured appropriately, this can be a difficult way to make good money.

FIXED FEE OR STRAIGHT DESIGN FEE

Many firms who know their area of specialty charge or bid on straight design fees. These may or may not include extra costs such as prints, travel, etc. Today more and more jobs are sold on a fixed-fee basis. The designer prepares designs, writes specifications, and may or may not oversee the project. They may be responsible for all or only one or two parts of the job. This works well in specialty areas where firms know the project and the client very well. It can be very profitable if managed properly. With profit, there is always a risk.

This fee can be a fixed/set amount or based on an hourly or per-diem basis. This fee is established by usual means, such as a review of the hours needed or cost of each staff member working on the project.

PER-SQUARE-FOOT CHARGE

A dollars-per-square-foot charge is appropriate to many projects. Space planning is often priced this way. The range is extensive and depends on the specialty. This is often used for comparison pricing to see if the project is within range.

REWARDS OF VALUE-BASED FEES

I think that the person who can complete a project fast and well deserves to be paid equally, or perhaps even more, than the person who took seventy hours or much longer for providing a lesser or equivalent quality project. Your experience in that specialty may mean that you do a better job in forty hours than they can in seventy. I suggest you charge according to the value of the project, rather than on an hourly fee.

RETAIL OR CONTRACTED PRICE

The retail or contracted method of charging means the design firm is responsible for delivering the project and all products for a set fee or a given price. At one time, the term for this was retail, and meant that designers charged a standard retail markup. Today the most-used term is "set contract price" since markups vary considerably. This may include all materials needed, as well as the delivery charges and any other costs required to complete the project.

The markups on this method of charging vary according to the requirements for the furniture and furnishings. These require greater overhead or a greater markup.

DESIGN CONCEPT FEE

This fee is a set amount for developing the initial design concept. The fee is paid for ideas on the development of the conceptual objectives of a project. Compensation is usually on a contracted or on a lump-sum basis, because it is the core of the design. Some firms may charge on an hourly or per-diem basis, or include the concept as a phase of the total project. This varies considerably, depending on the design specialty or the firm's style of working.

This method of charging is popular in areas where design centers are easily accessible. The clients can visit the center and see the prices. Many designers were initially forced to use this method, but now choose to use it, since they find it more professional and more profitable.

Today, concept development is often easy to sell for a good price, as it is something the client knows he can't do himself. He wants a great job—something different—and expects to pay high level fees for that special quality job.

At one time, firms would use this as a loss leader, keeping the design concept fee low, to enable them to build a relationship with the client and sell the rest of the project. Today, in this very competitive world, this often backfires. Clients can find sources for many of the items specified. If you have a specialty where clients cannot easily purchase the products themselves, this may still work well.

Designers today are finding that this up-front area, this area which has the sizzle, is what must generate the profit.

We must charge in areas where clients are willing to pay. Even though we know that the project management may be the key to this particular job, we may have to take a lesser fee for this phase because the clients think it's not of great value.

DESIGN-CONCEPT FEE PLUS PERCENTAGE—MIXED FEES

Some firms charge a design-study fee plus a percentage of the cost of furnishings, whether purchased directly from the firm or from other sources. This will vary according to the size of the project and the various responsibilities the firm handles on the project. For mid-sized to smaller residential or residentially detailed contract work, the percentages usually run somewhere between 25 and 40% of the cost of merchandise.

On residential work and small contract jobs, many designers work for a design-concept fee plus a percentage of cost of the items that are to be purchased or to be supervised. This percentage may apply to both construction items and furniture and accessories.

PERCENTAGE OF COST

Charging a percentage based on cost (or a percentage off the list price) is very popular in the contract field especially in respect to office furnishings. Clients are accustomed to this. If you mark up an item by 25 percent and the client is charged for receiving, warehousing and so on, the totals are within a few dollars of those charged for offering a typical 20 percent off the list, which is the norm. Sometimes it's not just a question of how you calculate it, but what clients are accustomed to seeing. They may think that a discount off retail is much better than a mark-up based on cost.

PERCENTAGE OF COST

An interior designer can provide his or her complete services including furnishings and labor, at cost, adding a fee based on a percentage of the total cost. With this method the design firm makes all purchases and passes onto the client all discounts, commissions and savings. The client thus obtains merchandise at a wholesale price plus the designer's fee. This fee will vary considerably depending on the type of work that is being performed. Obviously, the larger the job, the smaller the percentage of the fee must be. When firms charge an hourly fee plus a percentage of cost, the client needs to be clearly informed that project management and follow-up on problems usually represent a large portion of the fee—from one-third to one-half of the total.

FEE PLUS PERCENTAGE OF SAVINGS

This fee may be based on any of several other methods: straight fee, hourly, etc., plus a percentage of savings. For example: If the project cost is estimated at $500,000, and you are able to bring it in for $440,000, the owner may agree to split the difference with you on a 50/50 basis. More of these incentive programs are being developed because clients can see and understand their value. This method makes it worthwhile for the interior designer to try to plan the project in a price-effective way.

VALUE-BASED FEES

Value-based or straight design fees are based on what this job is worth in a particular market. In a very competitive market, you may have to develop ways of completing these projects quickly to stay competitive.

Clients like to know how much the project will cost. Whether we are talking about residential or contract work, I think that a straight fee or a value-based fee is best for the client, and best for the design firm. Of course, it's only good if you know exactly what you're doing, which is why that Design Service Outline is so important. You must establish exactly what you are doing on this project, and you need on-the-job experience to determine the appropriate costs.

Value-based fees (or value-oriented fees) are similar to straight design fees, but sold according to value. Some projects have special value, in that they are not routine, but have distinctive appeal. Example: Experts who know the fine points of a particular type of design can do great things because they know the specialty inside and out. They can also do it faster and at lower cost than a general practice firm. They are due the same fee, or even more, than a general practice firm. After all, they do a better job. This type of charging should be the aim of a firm who has the ability and the management process to assure high level creative design work in a specialized area.

A value-oriented fee commands a lump sum for a particular project. Lump-sum fees are usually profitable and often the best way of charging when the firm has done a lot of similar projects, knows the client, and has a good idea of their anticipated time expenditures. Designers who deal in specialties generally work on this basis because they have certain parts predesigned and can therefore complete a job very cost-effectively.

The best way of charging is with value-oriented fees. This has a high risk, but it also offers excellent opportunities for profit. If you understand the project and you run an efficient design firm, this method can be controllable and profitable. If the project is in an area in which you are unfamiliar, however, it can prove to be a loss.

Today, many design firms combine methods. They may charge a time + expenses fee for developing a concept, then set a fixed fee for the final phases once the project is determined. Some charge a fixed fee for the concept development plus a percentage of cost of merchandise purchased.

RETAIL OR SPECIALITY COMPANIES

Today traditional furniture stores are gradually being replaced by specialty stores or design galleries. Many clients want to buy a product, and retail organizations respond to that need. With good design service too, these businesses can be outstanding.

Some designers use a retail shop as a marketing tool; it is a comfortable way for a new client to get to know the designer and still feel in control. The retail method enables a client to think that he or she knows exactly how much the whole thing will cost; many residential clients understand product costs rather than fees. To the client who wants to have fun buying, this method will always remain attractive.

Retail or specialty companies usually have better buying methods for a specific group of items. Since they deal with a limited amount of resources, it gives them higher purchasing power, which enables them to deliver at a better price, faster, and with fewer delivery problems than a typical design firm could do. They have chosen their preferred vendors, given them a large quantity of business, and therefore can expect certain considerations.

DESIGNERS AS PURCHASE AND INSTALLATION COMPANIES

The firm may have one division that designs and then another that purchases, or they may only have one division that will purchase or purchase/install. This is prominent; the hospitality field is a specialty where this works.

KEYS TO SUCCESS

Keep your methods of charging simple, clear, and easy to calculate. This makes it easy for clients to understand.

Give yourself a financial base sufficient to allow for quality design development. It takes time to be truly creative—to really do a great job.

Design a profitable, but fair, structure that allows for flexibility where variables occur. A project changes as it grows.

Plan and aim to feature this client as a life-long patron.

No matter how you decide to charge, structure your fees so that they are easy for you to manage. Look at your services and what you are offering right now and take note of the areas where you have problems. Can you reorganize those portions of it to make your fee structure simpler for you to manage and easier for the client to understand?

BILLING PROCESS

Review your way of calculating costs to determine how you can structure it to complement your design work. This will give you that little bit of extra profit to reinvest in your practice, ensuring that you can maintain your standards.

Mixing fee styles—fee plus percentage or hourly rate plus percentage—often works for higher-level profitability. The design stars can dictate their fees, but most of us must find ways to make our fees palatable.

The process can make or destroy a job. Consider billing a client as certain parts of projects are completed. Consider the style of installation when arranging billing terms. Will the job be done in parts or all at once? Your structure for payment must be complementary. Look at your costs, look at your overhead, and also develop an understanding of what your clients are accustomed to seeing within this market and then try to tailor your fees accordingly. There are consultants who will help independent designers with this.

SCHEDULE PAYMENTS

The way you structure client payments on the project is critical to the ease of managing the job. Have the clients pay for phases rather than by the hour. For example:

PHASE	EXPECTED % OF FEE USED	CHARGE FOR
Data collection & evaluation; research and development	15%	20%
Design concept	15%	30%

Note: You have 50 percent of the fee, but you have only spent 30 percent of the time. If the clients are comfortable with this, and most firms find that they are, you have a good cash flow. If anything should happen to the project, you can walk away without feeling quite as injured as you would have without this financial cushion.

As you follow through your other phases, you will see the amount of your precentage reverse:

Project management	35%	25%

Clients think this area is easy and often object to paying for its true value. However, you know that project management is important; therefore, you want to do it in a way that ensures the finished project comes out exactly as planned. So allow for this loss up front.

Make a list of all areas that are to be worked on and the appropriate percentage of time to expend. Then create a pricing sheet for the client, based on phases completed and fee expected. It makes it easy to understand when to collect, and provides a safeguard.

BE PREPARED WITH FINANCING ARRANGEMENTS

Making it easy for people to buy from you is part of selling. Even though most of us do not want to be in the finance business, it often pays to be prepared to make financial arrangements for your clients if necessary. Some firms have earned more from their financial arrangements than from any other part of their business. To deal successfully with client finances, you need to establish good relationships with one or more banking institutions. There are many ways to develop financial structures and payment systems, and you must have it available for residential and corporate projects. Sometimes having financing available makes the difference between doing part of a project, or finishing it exactly as you feel it should be.

In today's market, financing is a changing system, so check with your banks regularly—at least every three months—to be sure you still have those options available.

Credit card systems, such as Design Access, are offered at many design centers. This credit system is based on your client's credit; the designer does not have any responsibility to pay if the client fails to pay. These cards allow clients to charge any purchase made within the design center. This assures immediate payment to both the suppliers and the design firms. Some banks offer MasterCard accounts on a large scale basis to permit designers to have credit available without the designer carrying the account. Given the present market, it will be meaningful to have many more creative methods of financing available. These financing methods contribute to keeping a good work flow.

Find a system of financing projects that works for you. Don't take this on yourself unless you are prepared to be in the finance business; most of us do not have the revenue—nor do we want—to be in the banking business.

ADJUSTMENTS

At times, for various reasons, designers are either forced to, or elect to, adjust billable hours or other items charged to a client. When you adjust the billing, be sure the clients are aware of it. Stamp the invoice in red so they can't help noticing that you gave them consideration.

The stamp may say in large print:
"Priority Client–No Charge"
    OR
"Priority Client–Reduced Fee"

Even your billing can be used for marketing and sales development. Enclose a reply card with your invoice asking for comments and feedback. This encourages clients' comments but should never replace your personal follow-up program.

BILLING TIPS
*Rewards:*Add a client advantage to the fee schedule. State the time you expect client communications will take. If the job is easier because client communication time is shorter

(not design or staff time) you may offer a deduction. For example:

> Design fee will include _____ (set fee).
> State all design phases.
> Review and consultation time—20 hours. Any additional time will be charged at the following rates. If the meeting time is less than 20 hours, you will be credited at the same rate.

This is an area which the clients can control. If they are prepared and make decisions at correct times, etc., you will find your work is easier. The benefit to the client is a lower consultation charge.

Another way to achieve the same client control is to say, "We expect the design planning phase of your project to take three months. If the support information and decision-making processes permit faster completion (within 60 days), the fee will be reduced by $5,000.00."

Start-up fee: If a project is delayed or stopped for any reason, a start-up fee or delayed fee may be needed to cover increased costs. (Refer to the chapter on contracts.)

Computer billings are often added to overhead expenses, since most design work stations have personal computers. In other situations, they are calculated separately, depending on the use.

ESTIMATE WITHIN RANGE

Estimates: Some special items are difficult to estimate. If you are concerned about cost, quote projects on a to/from price basis so they can expect a project to cost in the range of, for instance, $18,000 to $20,000. Make the top range high enough that you can be sure of bringing in the completed item for less. This gives you a cushion and makes you a hero if the item costs much less.

One year our accountant brought to our attention that the cost of merchandise purchased had increased eleven percent during that year. We had been used to very few increases in the prices of merchandise, and had always given our clients a firm quotation on all merchandise they were purchasing from us. We found that we had quoted below our normal mark-up range while our cost of merchandise and delivery had *increased* eleven percent. This caused us to lose money on many of our projects.

Often, when you buy merchandise you do not pay the listed price, but the price for the item on the day it is shipped to you. This can vary considerably from the amount you originally estimated. You should try to allow a ten percent variance in your estimates. For example, when you expect something to cost $4600, you should quote $4600 to $5200 so that you have some cushion in case there is an increase in price. If an item arrives in need of additional work or repair, you have the monies available to make adjustments and deliver the price just the way you want it. After all, the client *is* paying for your judgement.

CHARGING FOR THE INITIAL INTERVIEW

Should there be a charge for the initial interview? Whether a designer charges for the initial interview is a matter of personal choice. What are your purposes in an initial interview? Is it for marketing purposes? Does the prospective client just want a simple answer to a simple question, such as what color paint should be used if they are keeping all existing furnishings.

State your policy before visiting the project. Prospective clients seem to believe that designers exist for the sole purpose of having their minds picked. If you are going to give advice and want to charge for it, send out a written agreement along the lines of "We will review your reception room for the change of wallcovering. For that interview, our consultation fee will be $200." Ask the prospective client to sign and return it. This way, there is no misunderstanding by either party.

Firms have often said that they have had difficulty collecting for a simple consult handled by a staff designer or assistant. If you have billed for an interview that one of your staff or assistants has handled, it is likely that management has not structured this situation properly.

Stating your policy in advance will save a lot of aggravation. After all, many prospective clients have never purchased design services of any kind before. They don't really know how to buy design services, so help them by giving them the price tag in advance.

PROFIT ISSUES

The more creative or unusual the design specialty, the higher the profit can be. Today in the interior design market, the jobs with the highest profit are those that are the most innovative, the most unusual—ones that other people are not doing. To obtain the projects that permit innovation, a firm will often have to do a great deal of marketing research. This means that in the beginning jobs will principally be research-oriented and not necessarily profitable. When the firm develops skill in that unusual specialty, the profits increase. When competition enters the field, the profits start to drop until they reach the competitive bidding or cutthroat stage.

RETAINERS

Asking for a retainer or a deposit is important; it is part of the professional contract. In several states, designers have been discouraged from using the word "deposit" because, legally, a deposit must be placed in a separate escrow account for that client and cannot be mixed with funds of other projects. It is safe to call the advance a "retainer."

REPACKAGING YOUR SERVICES

There are three ways to get to the top of the heap. You can be truly innovative, which is the most difficult way. You can copy someone else at the top of the heap, which is also difficult. Or you can repackage your present types of services and give them a different name. By creating a new category of service, you make the fee scale more flexible. No one knows what the appropriate charge should be.

Find out what designers in your area are charging, and then decide what your rates need to be. You need to compare your costs to the market. In some areas you are limited by what the competition charges, unless you provide some service that no one else offers. In that case, you can name your own figure based on the value of the project.

No matter how you estimate your projects, the only way of being accurate is to make a comparison to your own past work. If you don't have a similar project for comparison purposes, then you need to speak with several other designers who have done similar jobs. For comparison, it is a good idea to figure the job several different ways and compare them; for example, per square foot versus hourly rate. This method can often pick up an error in your calculations.

When comparing a current project to a similar, past one, keep in mind that you should be able to complete it faster because you have experience in that area. Therefore, your costs should be less.

NEGOTIATION

Negotiation is often part of the pricing. Know what range will, and will not, work for this project. If the fee must be reduced, know what can be modified, eliminated or adjusted without putting your firm at a disadvantage. Let the client know what he or she will receive: prints, boards, specifications, real products, for instance. Your client should be made aware of the way you charge and the way you handle finances. When you present a fee schedule or a quotation to a client, it is important to give them an outline of all the services you will perform. If the client says the quotation is too high, you can indicate which areas can be eliminated.

ESTABLISHING THE DESIGNER'S HOURLY BILLING RATE

Example:

    Salary per year $24,000

    *Fringe benefits

     (35% of salary)   <u>8,400</u>

    DPE (direct

    personnel expense) $32,400 - 49 weeks =

$661.22 per week

If a designer works an average of 40 hours per week, the
usual number of chargeable hours is 30

        $661.22 - 30 hours - $22.04 per hour

Using a 2 1/2 to 3 1/2 percent multiplier, you can establish
an appropriate billing rate:

              2 1/2 = $55.00 per hour

              3   = $66.00 per hour

              3 1/2 = $77.00 per hour

*When calculating fringe benefits, include holidays, sick
leave, vacation, unemployment taxes, FICA, Workmen's
Compensation, insurance, and pension plan.

Figure 25-1

Chapter 26

The Installation

The installation is a very special opportunity to build a relationship. This takes place on their property. The clients can really see how much—or how little—you care. You resell a project to the client throughout its development. The way the installation is handled is key to obtaining additional work from the client, from their friends, and from other referrals. Since referrals make up a major portion of most design practices today, the way the client sees us is critical.

Organizing a polished installation takes time. Although we all prefer to do the complete installation at one time, it may not be your choice whether the installation is completed all at once, phased, or done a little bit at a time. But you can make the process less harrowing for the client in the way you organize and supervise the installers, and by planning ahead for problems.

Tell your contractors and craftspeople enough about the project so that they understand their roles and why things must be done in a certain way. To be sure they work well together, you should understand the processes involved in their jobs, and program the way they are to work together.

Go over the project with each craftsperson or delivery person three weeks before the installation and again four days ahead.

When you schedule an installation with a contractor, visit his or her warehouse and take inventory of each item needed for the project. Often a contractor will believe he is ready to go when in fact he has only ninety percent of what is needed—and that last ten percent can hold up your project. You must decide whether the contractor should go into the space without the necessary materials, whether to hold off, or to substitute.

Plan the installation so that each craftsperson and contractor can perform his or her role easily and with the least likelihood of damaging other parts of the project. This can be as simple as preventing a piece from being installed too soon.

If you are on a tight schedule, it can be cost-effective to have a well-paid project manager on site. This person must make decisions and adjustments to the project because a space is rarely exactly as you expect.

Sometimes a client will say that his or her office can handle the installation, but I try to discourage this. It is a rare client who understands installation procedures, and it only takes one careless installer to mar a project that may have taken months or years of careful effort on your part.

PREPARE THE SITE

Before the day of the installation, tell the building management the date and time you will start work and what your installation team will need. This can range from parking spaces and freight elevators to street closings. Hiring a traffic coordinator to direct people to a lot can be money well spent.

Check the site the day before installation to make sure it is clean and ready. Are the temperatures corect for installing carpet and other items? Is the HVAC system functioning properly?

Ask the client to avoid the site during the installation so that the person in charge is responsible and in full control. Specify appropriate times for the client to come and review or approve the process. It is vital for your firm that your representative be visibly in charge. Too often a contractor may point something out to the client, who, not knowing enough about the situation, may seem to approve. This allows the contractor to say, "But the client okayed it," should you object. All too often clients on site during installations become over-concerned with inappropriate details and increase the cost of the installation.

TIPS FOR A SMOOTH INSTALLATION

Be prepared. Go over the list of everything that is to be installed or to be done in the client's space. Make sure that it's done in an orderly fashion and that you have everything you need. Try to make your deliveries all at once so that the client gets the full impact of the design.

For any installation, give the clients an approximate time—morning or afternoon—when the craftspeople will arrive. Don't keep them waiting if you can help it; they probably have rearranged their schedules to be on site for you.

The behavior and appearance of contractors and craftspeople you hire reflects on you. Send only people who have reasonably good personalities, who will show a little interest in the client, and be friendly enough to put them at ease. If the designer in charge cannot be present, be sure that there is at least one person there whom the client has met before and is comfortable with. This person can introduce the others. When your staff and contractors enter a client's space, they should appear appropriately well-groomed and neat. As they are there to work, a three-piece suit is inappropriate, but so are filthy overalls at the beginning of the day.

Clients believe that their space is important. They want it kept clean and in order. Playing loud music, smoking, eating, and drinking in the installation area are out of the question. Let your installers know your ground rules before they reach the site. On a large project, create an area where they may take breaks, and see that it is cleaned up before you leave. Having coffee or sodas on hand and arranging for delivery of lunches can save you time and money.

Respect the client's space, whether it is a residential or a commercial project. Put down floor mats and floorcoverings when working. Ask the installers to be neat, or at least to try not to make any messes that cannot be cleaned up before they leave the space.

Vacuum cleaners, brooms, dustcloths, garbage bags, materials for touch-ups and minor repairs, and a stain-removal kit should be part of your standard installation equipment. When your installation crew leaves a space, even though they may be back the next day, that space should be clean.

Even if there is a member of your staff on site, ask each installer to call your office to confirm that he is on-site, and take note of the time. Make sure the installer also gives your office a status report on the site, especially if there are any difficulties. You might be told that the paperhanger isn't finished and won't be until the afternoon. Decide what you want the installer to do in the meantime. Adjustments to the installation schedule should be made by your office, not the individual installers.

As each installer finishes for the day, he or she should call your office so that the time can be noted.

INSTALLATION MAGIC

Make a show out of that installation. Rent a red carpet for furniture delivery when installing a larger project. All too often these are projects under construction and may not be as clean as one would like. Red carpets are available from any of the rent-it-centers at a very moderate cost. Rent enough to run from the van into the building, and roll out the red carpet as you open the truck doors.

Assign booties or shoe coverings to the furniture movers so that they do not mar the carpets or other floors in the space. They also can wear white gloves to ensure that no fingermarks or smudges are left on any piece of furniture or fabric.

Cover each piece of furniture with blankets and padding. This not only protects it, but camouflages the shapes. No one sees the furniture until it is in place and the wrapping is removed.

This kind of installation will have great impact on the neighborhood. Everyone will wonder what is happening at that office building or that residence. Your showmanship calls attention to your firm and sets it apart from any others in the area. Be sure the space is perfectly clean, that all pieces are perfect and at their best.

Ask your clients to give you the freedom of the property that day, and request that all their staff and/or family be out of the building during the installation. Schedule a time for their return, say, 4:00. Depending upon the client, you might serve a nice tea, or a bottle of champagne and appropriate refreshments. Whatever you do, make the installation special. Have flowers. Have an extra gift for them. Leave something on their desk that shows that your firm cares.

Installation and service during a project really build client rapport.

WHY EVERY PROJECT SHOULD INCLUDE A MAINTENANCE MANUAL

Would you clean an upholstered chair with a garden hose? To ensure that the client understands what constitutes everyday use, that the space maintains its optimum quality, and to safeguard your liability position, it is important to see that the client or end-user receives appropriate instructions on how to use and maintain the installed products.

The budgets we work with are high, and some items we specify are the result of technology so new that perhaps only the manufacturers and furniture designer completely understand them. For instance, very often the instructions to an active ergonomic desk chair are attached by the manufacturer to the chair itself. All too often these instructions are lost, either during installation or by the first user, while the chair remains in the space for many years.

A maintenance manual should provide the central location for documents and instruction booklets. It gives the client a reference, which can lessen the possibility of real problems due to misuse of the furniture. Also include any other information you know about the piece: how it should be handled, moved or adjusted. For landscape furniture, instructions for future disassembly and reassembly are important.

Cleaning instructions also belong in the maintenance manual. These are furnished by our resources, who may state that specific cleaners are required to maintain flameproof or fire retardant finishes, especially. Some pieces are sold with guarantees and restrictions. These too belong in the maintenance manual. It's acceptable to clean certain types of lawn furniture by turning loose a chimpanzee with a garden hose, but such treatment could invalidate the warranties and guarantees of most of the furniture and furnishings we specify.

In this manual you will want to list any preferred maintenance people, as well as red-flagging any issue, item or potential problem. By each red-flagged item, tell the client whether they should check with the design firm, the dealer/distributor or the manufacturer. For example, we installed a very elaborate stained glass ceiling that was best cleaned only by someone who is familiar with the structure. In the maintenance manual we specifically named that person, how the client could get in touch with him, and how often we recommended the item be cleaned.

WHAT THE MANUAL SHOULD CONTAIN

The information that goes in this maintenance manual should come from the manufacturers as much as possible; that way the designer acts as a vehicle for the distribution of information but is not directly responsible for the durability, wearability or breakdown of any particular part or component. All guarantees and warranties are automatically passed on to the client, as well as certificates for flame proofing or special finishes. This information may save you from being blamed for matters beyond your control.

The documents and instruction booklets come in a variety of sizes, and compiling the information is easier than presenting it. Your "manual" can be simple or complex, depending on the scope of the project. The "manual" is usually a standard 3-ring binder with envelope pockets and dividers. On the title page, you should put your firm name, address, and phone number.

In some instances, you may want to have the instructions photocopied onto standard pages. When you do this, be sure you also include the original document.

A maintenance manual not only lessens your liability, but it is good public relations and a marketing tool. The manual states what can legitimately be expected of certain items in terms of wear and probable length of time before they will need to be replaced. It gives the client a resource and a direction whenever they have additional needs, which means that they will be familiar with your office and prepared to call it when they add, change or alter their interior space. The client knows that if something happens to a chair after four or five years of use, it is not unusual but expected, and that there is an established maintenance procedure.

You should supply a maintenance manual to the client at installation time or immediately thereafter. It should list each and every piece of furniture, equipment, furnishings, and/or material incorporated in that project, including carpeting, wallcoverings, draperies, window treatments, furnishings, textiles, and lamps. A good manual lists handling precautions and cleaning and maintenance instructions, as well as the correct wattage for the lamping. It also includes the names, addresses and phone numbers of other companies to be called for service or additional instructions for adequate maintenance.

MAINTENANCE REVIEW SERVICE OR UPDATING

Some design firms make available to their clients a maintenance review service. This means that the design firm visits the project every six to twelve months, depending on the type of project, to review the installation and determine whether changes in the frequency and type of maintenance are necessary. At this time, the design firm can update the accessories and any other elements that need to be improved to keep the space state-of-the-art.

Design is a service business, and we need to be able to give our clients ongoing and continuing service. Our clients have invested in their interiors and want the appearance to reflect their investment. Industry predictions say that growth in the nineties will be based on service.

Maintenance manuals are a service, and a way to encourage a continuing and profitable relationship. The maintenance manual reminds clients of the designer who worked on their project, and that you take care of their interior space. This is, without question, the best marketing tool and the best reminder that you can have.

Installing a good job and maintaining it is good salesmanship.

POST-OCCUPANCY REVIEWS

Schedule post-occupancy reviews for thirty days, ninety days, six months, and a year after the project is installed. You may continue them longer, depending upon the project. Send a representative to the project to check on how well it is working. Document it. If there are problems, you know about them immediately. If everything looks fine and seems to be performing as it should for a year, and then a client calls and says, "This never worked," you know differently. You were there; you reviewed it with them. Everything functioned just beautifully at the time of the reviews.

FOLLOW-UP

After the project is finished, if you want the client to continue to be your client and not someone else's, find a way to keep in touch.

During the project you've been in constant touch with the client, sometimes on a daily basis. Don't stop cold when the project is finished. Instead you need a period of "weaning" where you may call every week. It is still a scheduled call, and gradually you decrease the frequency to every other week, three weeks, four weeks.

Later on, you should be in touch with past clients at least four to six times a year, every single year. Send birthday cards, articles you think they might enjoy, and updates on what your firm is doing. Try to find ways to promote your firm while also making the client feel they are still important to you.

Use the Past Client Follow-Up Summary to document your contacts. This follow-up process will reap many rewards.

Past Client Follow-Up Summary

Client: _____ Contact Person: _____

Address: _____ Position: _____

_____ Phone Number: _____

Finish Date:	Job:	Type: (room or building)	Size:

Last Contract Date:	Client's Comments:	Follow-through:

Figure 26-1

Chapter 27

Learning

Being a good designer today means continual education. What should you know to make yourself the designer you want to be? There is only one way to find out and that's to expose ourselves to various learning opportunities. According to Peter M. Singe (The Fifth Discipline, Doubleday, Currency, NY, 1990), for a company to be successful today, it must be a learning environment; education has to be part of the company structure.

Learning needs to be a part of the whole company's program, and to be successful, it has to start with the top management structure. If the people in management are not ready to learn, if they don't recognize that they need new material, it's very hard to convince the employees they should take their Saturday or their off-time and dedicate it to education. So it must start with the top.

Everyone needs to be exposed to new material. Everyone within a firm has a role to play in marketing and selling that firm, so marketing and sales training is for everyone. Just as we want and need to learn more about design issues, we also need exposure to methods of building client relationships, sales, and marketing. Our clients are studying. Our competition is studying. Our clients know when we are doing our job correctly.

Learning experiences also help prevent burn-out. These refresh and renew the excitement and motivation we felt as students. Schedule regular growth experiences for your staff to get out and learn new material. Promote an environment that promotes learning in your firm; make it an important issue.

How do you get this training? Attend seminars or arrange to have a coach or a consultant to come in. The important thing is to make the investment and invest in the type of learning structured to teach your people what they need to know. Bring a consultant into your firm. An outside specialist can say things to your staff that would not be accepted as well if they came from you or other people in the firm with whom they work on an everyday basis. So often, this outside consultant can really cut through to the issue.

To determine what your firm needs to learn, it's a good idea to write down your objectives to see what the needs and problems are. Review your goals. What additional knowledge or abilities do you need to meet? What is your competition going to be and how can you best compete? What are the major issues that you need to improve and how can you acquire this information?

Depending upon the type of information you need, you will then want to determine whether it's something that could be covered in a seminar, which your competition (this is also a way to learn about them) also may attend, or whether you need to go beyond your community to attend a seminar or a program where you can have interaction from other areas. One great advantage of attending seminars is that you are exposed to the issues by many different design companies, giving you a wider exposure than you could get from the seminar leader alone. Also, there is networking value in attending seminars.

Encourage your staff to make the most of their seminar experiences by requesting that anyone who is sent to a seminar or a program keep an outline of exactly what they learned, and another of how that information can be used in your firm. What can be used now, and what applies to future situations? Ask for a priority list.

Schedule a special staff meeting at which the person who attended the seminar can tell the rest of your firm about it. This does several things. First, it encourages the seminar attendee to listen carefully. Second, reviewing this information for presentation reinforces the learning. Creating a priority list puts the lesson into usable format.

LEARN FROM OTHERS

We can't originate everything ourselves, and sometimes our ways of doing things may be more complex than is necessary. So look at how other people are doing things and borrow from them. It's faster to polish someone else's method than to invent a new technique. Find the best person you can find to emulate. Take what you can from their ideas and processes, and polish them and develop them to fit your own way of working.

When you need to develop a special technique, ask other designers if they know anyone who has had a similar problem and how it was handled. Most of the issues in this book are the result of questions designers asked me, which later were reviewed with many professional consultants. The suggestions are tested in several design firms and, when they work, recorded so they can be repeated.

Keep studying, researching, and learning. This is how we grow. This is why we have consultants, this is why we go to seminars: we need to know more about our field. Experience can teach us a lot, but it is much less expensive to find a consultant who has done it before and learn from them. It can build the speed of your progress considerably. Find people to whom you can relate and whom you enjoy being around, and learn from them.

Learn from others. They know how they want to be treated.

Demonstrate sincere caring. This is worth more than anything you can buy.

Help your clients realize their great potential through appropriate interior design. Make them look great.

Realize the excitement of knowledge. Study and learn. Improvement and success starts with ability. Today it takes constant training.

Take the time necessary to build the proper relationship with clients. Only the right one will give you the basis for doing that right job.

Our consultants, sources, craftsmen are what make us. Without them we cannot do interior design.

Fortunately, you learned enough in school to get a job in design. But keeping that job depends on what you continue to learn from your present teachers, clients, consultants, sources, and craftspeople.

Suggested Reading List

Carnegie, Dale. 1981 *How to Win Friends and Influence People.* New York, NY. Pocket Book.

David, Stanley M. 1987 *Future Perfect.* Reading, MA. Addison Wesley Publishing.

DePree, Hugh. 1986 *Business As Usual.* Zeeland, MI., Herman Miller.

Harrington, H. James. 1988 *The Improvement Process. How America's leading companies improve quality.* McGraw-Hill.

Healy, William J. and Gottleib, Marion. 1990 *Making Deals. No-lose negotiating—the new standard.* Simon & Schuster.

Johnson, Spencer and Blanchard, Ken. 1982 *The One Minute Manager.* New York, NY. William Morris & Company.

Marcus, Stanley. 1974 *Minding the Store.* Boston, Little Brown & Company.

Marcus, Stanley. 1979 *Quest for the Best.* The Viking Press, New York, NY.

Naisbitt, John and Aburdene, Patricia. 1990 *Megatrends 2000.* New York, NY. William Morrow & Co.

Peters, Tom and Austin, Nancy. 1985 *A Passion for Excellence.* New York, NY. Random House.

Peters, Tom. 1987 *Thriving on Chaos.* New York, NY. Alfred Knopf.

Singe, Peter M. 1990 *The Fifth Discipline. The art and practice of the learning organization.* Currency, New York. Doubleday.

Stanley, Dr. Thomas J. 1991 *Selling to the Affluent. The rich are different from you and me.* Irwin. Business One.

Toffler, Alvin. 1985 *Powershift.* New York, NY. Random House.

Zemke, Ron and Schaff, Dick. 1989 *101 Companies That Profit From Customer Care.* NAL Inc.

Index